FLYING WITH SEAGULLS

(Rituals Of The Mind)

A Volume Of Poems To Tickle The
Heart And The Mind.

THOMAS P. LIND

FLYING WITH SEAGULLS

ISBN 978-0-9800989-0-7

LIND PUBLISHING 210 Foxwood Dr. Brandon, Florida 33510-4013, Ph/Fax 813 681 2551. mailto:tom.lind@live.com **All rights reserved under International Law.**

Table of Contents

DEDICATED TO

THAT SPECIAL YOU

Stop taking yourself for granted.
You are the luckiest person
In the whole world. You are unique!
There never was, and never will
Be, another person like you.

.

Consider probability,
The laws of chance involved with you
To form the color of your hair,
The smile, and the gleam in your eyes.
None in a million is like you.

You have won the lottery of life,
Don't spend it recklessly in strife.
You only have one shot at life,
There are no other prescriptions,
No exchanges, no more refills.

Sit, watch the stars and enjoy them,
Wonder what else you could have been.
Marvel in wonderment your luck,
One sperm picked a special ovum
And you became the star of stars!

The odds to the highest power
Are more than astronomical
To be conceived at that hour,

To change the world by what you think.
You are relevant—important!

THE ROSE AND THE WIND

The storm thundered around the crooked lane
Clipping green leaves of grass and roses too,
Fallen upon the sandy grains of lost yesterdays.
It was not the storm to blame, nor the fallen.
The fallen rose, which fell from warped caresses
Of disproportional care clipped and snapped!
The foursome wind laughing, moved in swirling steps
To face the indifferent elm planted before the
Seasons of disrepair. The gardener howled the cry of
Simulated childbirth, the rose and the wind were dead!

PREFACE

Existence is a reflection from the kaleidoscope of our imagination.
Every turn is a quantum leap ever changing!

The history of our development has its black holes and hidden secrets from which it is difficult to find a clear way out. The period of the renaissance provided a window and a means to escape from the vestiges of lost creeds and doctrines, which became rampant after the fall of the Roman Empire. From many writers emerged the traces of what was to become a Humanistic Philosophy. A view that gives us the right perspective about our humanity; this opened the doors for other writers we call existentialist—or existentialism. However, there are many who still cannot emerge from the darkness of the dark ages. Emerge from the dark holes of history and see the light at the other end of the tunnel.

Humanism and its developments lead us to existential thought, which, in effect, is the foundation for a new world view, and our place in the Universe—a new philosophy of freedom of the mind, the soul and of the will, which has changed how we govern ourselves and live—the era of enlightment. Those still holding on to pre-renaissance thoughts think that humanism and existentialism are the great evils of our time, that's because these philosophies expose their Dark Age and medieval thinking. They would rather live with myths, and fantasies and mysteries, than face the realism—the fact and reality of life—our humanistic and existential position in the Universe.

The evils we are facing in the world today came from the twisted thoughts imposed on us by those who set themselves up as authorities, wanting to control our minds and souls.

These people reflecting their narrow frame of mind would like to hold us in time, carrying us back to the dark ages, to live in squalor, poverty and disease. What they promise us is a reward in some imagined future heaven, of which they have no proof, but is only an assumption in their crazy heads. I do not know about you, but I like my freedom of mind, of will. I like to roam the earth free, as it is intended to be. I like to freely eat of the fruits I see, and inhale a fresh breath of air.

The job of a social critic is to analyze not to criticize, and to find solutions where possible. With that intent, we must ask why: Doctrines of the past, doctrines of obscurantism with the sinister objective to keep us in the dark, in ignorance, have always existed, and allowed to exist, even today? The peddlers of these doctrines would compel us to fall on our knees and denigrate ourselves. Worship their alter egos. Their arrogance overshadows the grandeur of the vestures they assume and parade in. They want us to be penitent for transgressions we have not committed. Brainwash us with rhythmic hypnotic chants to believe histories that have no relevance to our human need in the here and now.

If we are to recognize anything it is Human Dignity, and our responsibility for others and us—these people haven't the slightest idea of what this means—what I am talking about. It is irresponsible to hold an ideology that degrades humanity. It is degrading to crucify children before they are born, and to burden them not only with economic debt, but also with guilt for all eternity. This gets to be an emotional issue with those promoting and spreading these doctrines—it's hard to find their motives, and define their emotions. Why? We cannot find any logic, nor they give a reason, except that they themselves are the victims of their own confused thoughts. The only certainty is that they will kill everyone who does not believe as they do. Some people take their scriptures for science, which through the ages has had devastating result. To live with fallacies of our making is but to live a fool's life.

In a free democratic society, we respect the sentiments and opinions of other people, and we expect them to respect ours. However, because we do, that doesn't mean we should accept them and make them our own, or that they are necessarily true. We must also look at this from a global general prospective, if we are holding on to certain opinions from generations, does that make these opinions true? It only means that these opinions are promulgated from generations to generation without question. And there was a time in our history that if we questioned those in authority, they would put us on the rack and torture us to death.

What we are questioning here, are those factions in our societies through the world that still promote this punishment for none-believers. They strap bombs to their brainwashed disciples, and send them to kill thousands of innocent people. And they do it because they believe there is a reward for them in heaven. If we can see the irony here, why can't we see it in all the other insidious ideas we are promoting? Can we see the devastation we are bringing to the world by trying to impose our unfounded opinions on others? The result of this indoctrination has corrupted our minds in all walks of life. I could not believe this, but here is a shocker for our enlightened world: In surveys taken, 66% of the people surveyed worldwide believe in Satan. More believe in ghosts, and a spiritual world—many believe we can talk to the dead and the dead sends messages back to us. Now here is another shocker, of this 66% many are educated people, professors, physicians, attorneys, and of course the theologians. (The holy righteous, believe they are mightier than the sword, and will not spare the sword to impose the errancy of their views.) No human is infallible! No matter what rank we give them, or what rank they may assume.

There is so much that we don't know and much more that we cannot know, that's why we rationalize, that's why we make unfounded assumptions. And many of us, figuratively speaking, do jump off the cliff—we make leaps of faith. Only few of us are lucky to fall back where we were standing unhurt.

Religion, science, philosophy and psychology have been too concerned with essentials, that is, with the essential parts that make a human being. It is the total organism as a person that exists—the person that exists in time and space; that perceives problems in relationships with other existing organisms. It's the total perceiving organism in relationship that should be our epistemological concern. This concern with essentialist metaphysics has compounded our problem of existing, drawn us away from confronting the pragmatism of our everyday physical lives. That physical life of course includes our mental and emotional lives as well. However, none is essential without the other.

A concern with essence is a throwback to the philosophies of Plato, Aristotle and Aquinas. Essence and necessity contradict free choice—the essential and the necessary sets us up not only in a philosophical box, but also to a life of restrictions and obligations. Existentially we must make a distinction between obligation and duty. Obligation is something we are legally and morally bound to do. Whereas duty is something we voluntarily assume to do. We take the responsibility for doing—we have a choice. It would help us to respect this distinction; it doesn't mean there are no moral consequences. Choice is moral; there is no morality without choice.

Man is problematic to himself, because he does not understand his existential position, which is to accept responsibility for life—his life. It is a duty not an obligation. He is not obligated, but whatever, he does have moral consequences. Without making a commitment to himself, he cannot live a moral and ethical life. Morality is utilitarian. This is not meant in a selfish way, for the commitment is to life. Even so, life only becomes meaningful and purposeful through the individual—we each lives in a vast expanse of "nothingness" behind us, ahead and around us, which has no intrinsic or extrinsic meaning for us. Meaning and purpose come to us from the reality, we produce in consciousness. Truth is only in the reality we can conceive, perceive. And we only believe that to which we have made a commitment. So if we make a commitment to life, we can believe in ourselves, and live as close to the truth as we produce it in action.

If we make a commitment to something above and beyond life we make a commitment to a fantasy, which cannot be translated to an existential reality. This is what produces our ontological doubt, and our loss of sense of "being". We lose our potential to guide our own destiny. We must become centered and self-possessed to understand our position in the scheme of existence, and take control of our lives and guide our own destiny. As humans there is no other destiny but that which we can conceive for us, and to which we make a commitment. No one is responsible for this but us. Sentimentalism is not necessary, but it can be good if it is adding spice to our lives, and we use it only to the extent it does not interfere with living purposeful and fruitful lives.

From an ontological point of view and a cosmological perspective everything, we think and say about the Universe and us is an assumption and a rationalization. From an existential point of view if we take conscious life as integral and necessary to the phenomenon of the Universe, we can give meaning and purpose to our existence. This can help us to define the Universe. But first we must define ourselves. This has presented an insurmountable task to philosophy, science and psychology. Of course theologians think they have all the answers, disregarding logic and all the inconsistencies in their theories and theologies.

There were two major discoveries that we finally accepted, that have helped us to define the Universe and our position. The first was, that the world is not flat, that we live on a round planet; the second, that we are not the center of the Universe. In fact, we are just one small planet among billions of others, revolving in a tiny corner of our galaxy, among billions of other galaxies. The Universe does not revolve around us, we revolve around the sun, without which life would not have evolved, and continued. The third we need to help us define our existence is conscious life. We have to accept, that conscious life is integral and necessary to the Universe. Without which there would not be an existence, as we know it. It took many battles, blood and tears for us to accept discoveries one and two. We tore down many walls. We are now many years into the future when we fought those battles. And we consider ourselves enlightened and civilized. How hard do we have to fight today, how much blood and tears we have to shed, how many lives do we have to sacrifice to accept discovery three?

Discovery one and two were revolutionary, causing upheavals in our way of thinking and society, opening new worlds, new directions in knowledge and developments in science. Let's ask ourselves this question: what would have happened if we were not able to change the minds of the people who thought the world was flat, and that the Universe revolved around us? We would not have discovered America, and no shuttle flight from Cape Canaveral to outer space! What do you think will happen when we accept the proposition that without conscious beings throughout the Universes, there is no existence, as we know it? Is this too futuristic? Is this too hard an idea to grasp? It needs a new revolution in our way of thinking—a paradigm shift in understanding the Universe and our position towards it. Consider the medieval views, and the views we have now, and what our future will be, when we make that paradigm shift.

Neo-Platonism was perhaps a development over the Platonist school of thought, but not an improvement and we find many traces in the background of our thought. It talks about creative activity and pure intelligence. This is not what we are talking about when we talk about consciousness, because intelligence is only one of the functions that arise out of consciousness. The rationalism of René Descartes has not helped us much either, we cannot live by reason alone, we know that logic can be faulty, if we start with the wrong premise. We need all of our other mental faculties and emotions—we must feel what we think and think what we feel.

I have said above that man is problematic to him. We must understand this not only philosophically, but also practically. First, he is part of a collective humanity with its many problems of development and surviving—the human problem. Second, he is an individual, as an individual, he must deal with the personal dimensions of what it means to be human. That is, his physical, mental, emotional, sexual and economic life; and, his dealings with other humans, other spices, and the physical environment around on which he depends. Collectively humanity has not done so well. All I have to say is, we still have corrupt governments, devastating wars, unbelievable religions, ignorance, hatred, poverty and incurable diseases—we haven't solved the human problem! Individually there are many outstanding successes—that is, individuals who have learned to live life successfully. Unfortunately, also as individuals, there are so many failures.

Humanism and existentialism are a neo-rationalism that cuts and goes beyond all the make-beliefs, the myths and superstitions that we have been living with for so long. It is an understanding, and accepting our position in the Universe. An understanding of the human factor as necessary to the evolving universe—other existences are determined in time by the evolutionary position of other conscious intelligent entities throughout the other Universes. However, that's another story. Our tasks should be to solve the political and psychological entanglements we are in and the dynamics of our physical and spiritual needs here on earth.

I hope this will help to set the emotional tone to enjoy the poems in the volume,

Tomas P. Lind,
Brandon, Florida, 2012

PREDULE

Poetry is a symbolic representation of an absolute,
Of the intuitive grasp of something great,
We don't know quite how to express,
The foundation of imagination unencumbered.

The expression of a smile, the face of a newborn
Conveys but a hint of that greatness within.
Imagination in its entire ramifications in
Poetry humbly captures every subtle line.

From prehistoric time to the present and the unforeseeable future, we have expressed and will express our joys and sorrows, achievements and disappointments, wars and reconciliation, and above all, love and die by the rhythm and rhyme of poetry. Why? Because life itself is a metaphor and we live and die by simile and analogy. There is nothing in the Universe more similar and unlike than a human. Life itself is poetry and drama at the same time, and each person is a living poem. Our lives may not rhyme all the time, there may be discords, and free style living, but there is rhythm in the up and down, the rise and fall—the mood swings when we love and hate—laugh and cry! It's this rhythm that makes life bearable—a big sigh.

Is it any wonder then why poetry is the oldest artistic form of expression and communication? It was the first form of self-expression used to record and tell about our wanderings. What we were discovering about our world and ourselves.

Poetry has always been hard to define, because it's not something we know, but what we feel. All our feelings are abstract, and like poetry, any definitions we may give them are at best approximations. The best way to express an abstract idea, or a feeling, is by analogy and metaphor. Although when we are in deep sorrow and anguish we may not think so, but when we are happy, we see the sun shining everywhere. We also like to live our lives by contrast. These are the same devices by which great poems are created.

As an art form, poetry has a place in the minds and hearts of many people, who enjoy and derive much pleasure from reading poetry. However, it has its own share of controversy, as so many of the other art forms. Much about this has been written over the years, eloquently. One main refrain comes from people who say they don't read poetry because they do not understand it. And some say they don't derive any value reading poetry. What these people are saying is that poetry is not pragmatic and utilitarian but isn't this also the same songs, we hear about all the other art forms?

I would like for us to take some time out and consider, ultimately. What is life all about? If we can answer this question honestly, we may get a better idea of what it means to be pragmatic and utilitarian. What is it that ultimately life has to offer us? I mean this seriously, realistically, without the make-belief. What is it? We are searching for? All the things we accumulate and do—what are they supposed to do for us? I think we all know the answer and it's pragmatic and utilitarian: They do not give us contentment and peace, not even lasting comfort and happiness. Is life then worth the effort? The answer is yes, if we want to be pragmatic and utilitarian. We must not forget that we have this great ability to give life meaning and purpose. This is what art does for us; it helps to make life enjoyable and meaningful.

One of the best descriptions of a poem I have read, if we can call it that, is from Archibald MacLeach (1892-1982)

American poet: In "Ars Poetica". Collected Poems 1917-1952
(Boston: Houghton, Mifflin, 1952)
MacLeish use metaphors, contrasting imagery and declarative
sentences to our great delight, as follows:

"A poem should be palpable and mute
As a globed fruit

Dumb
As old medallions to the thumb

Silent as the sleeve-worn stone
Of casement ledges where the moss has grown—

A poem should be wordless
As the flight of birds

A poem should be motionless in time
As the moon climbs

A poem should not mean
But be."

In other words, what he is saying is that a poem should "Be"
not say. That is perhaps good advice for all of us. It's what
the poem does to the reader and what the reader does to the
poem that's important. It's like the scientific description of a
sunset (Pragmatic) it does nothing for the reader; but let us
behold a sunset, we become emotionally stirred with awe and
wonder.

This is exactly what poetry is supposed to do for us,
cut through the intelligible meaning, and stirs our souls to the
core. The poem then has a personal meaning, and becomes

associated with us through the power of its own "being". It's an association arrived at without the benefit of logic and reasoning. That does not mean however, that the poem must not be logical and intelligently constructed. This in itself should suffice describing what poetry is.

Poets also have been accused of being obscure. Whether a poet is obscure or not is an academic question. However, as far as the general reader is concerned the question resolves itself into a practical one (Utilitarian), and it is contingent on many factors. First the reader, the reader must read poetry with an open heart if not an open mind; then the poet: Poets become obscure when they use imagery and symbols, which have meaning and connotation only to themselves—poets can be out of touch—living in the castles of their own imagination, fighting Quixote-like battles, but this can be more of a virtue than a fault, for imagination is that the supreme faculty, we have that projects us beyond the jungles, and widen our horizons. It creates light from the obscurity of non-existence.

Poets also make philosophical statements, but the intent is not mere philosophy, it is more to enriching our emotional lives. (I am thinking of Dante here.) The poet's task is to be in touch with the sentiments of his era, and stir the heartthrob of the people he is singing to. Every poem written is an attempt to solve the mysteries of life— or at least to live them, and share them with someone.

Poetry has been significant in the development of the human experience. It has help shape our collective and individual history. From the very early mirroring of our self-awareness, a mirroring of our aspirations, achievements, disappointments, downfalls, our anguish, and above all our joys and the "Aha" experience!

Now that we have explored some problems of poetry, poets and the reader, we should be in a better position to browse through a few works of poetry and choose the ones suited to our temperament. The experience we gain from reading poetry will certainly bring a cadence into our lives, which will enrich us.

What I like about writing poetry is that it let's my mind flow free, and pretty soon a mood, I am able to see, which I write down on paper for someone to feel. I see long and short words dancing to the rhythm of my pen. They cut up on the paper, prancing, for everyone to see. They keep on dancing a formal tango or just waltzing, hitting the floor break dancing, hip hoping along to a swing. The important thing is to get in the mood and swing, and sing and dance. Don't be critical of all the jumping steps and cutting up on the floor, go with the rhythm and the flow. If reading this your mood swings from blue to glad, and sends you dancing, prancing on the streets, an emotion has been conveyed to you. You are free to share it with everyone you know. Now you should be in the mood for singing, in rhythm with the poems in this book!

SPEAKING TO YOUR CONCERNS

My silence is not dumb,
Or mute to my inner ear;
Nor my solitude empty,
Replete with ethereal air—
Poems filled atmosphere!

Speaking to your concern,
Conceived in my inner world,
Where our worlds surely collide—
We meet ever to depart.

This is where we all discern,
Life is like a Ferris wheel,
It has no destination—
The ride ends where it begins.

A silent witness speaks not,
But wonders at the Charade.
Many suns do not go down,
Nor the moons play hide and seek,
And the sea waves crest no more.
Somewhere all has lost its splendor—
That is, all that man has made!

How do we know, what we know?

How to reach the discontent,
Not living within them.
The mirror of life reflects
The state of our mental world—
Also, our religious bent.

The expectancy of the unreal,
Leads to the surreal,
Melancholy is misery,
It opens the gates to nowhere.

The "truth" of the world revealed.
Life has no destination,
The pleasure is the journey—
The moon does reflect the sun,
Its brilliance is our view!

WHEN WE STOP TO THINK

When we stop to think,
it's the mind that matters
from the dawn of civilization
to the present day.
First, we swing from limb to limb,
and learned rivers to swim.
We just didn't awake one morning
the newspapers reading.
Second, learned to upright walk,
going through the forests screaming
destroying every living thing.
But the forest fires lightning lit
scared us beyond our wit,
until a Flintstone accidentally hit
we learn fire lighting of our own,
many things burning we hadn't grown.
It was some kind of awakening,
pause for reflection an insight gained,
when we saw our image in a stream
it dashed us down the pit of hell,
wondered what could that be
peering back frowning or grinning.
That's when we started thinking.
This thinking that was thinking
these crazy thoughts we hadn't known.
It seems to be the cause of inspiration,
wondering what's the cause of creation.
These thoughts of themselves racing
through the forest and the skies,
saw dragons, ghosts, gods and gremlins,
standing on the sole of our feet trembling.

Some time thereafter we learn, not fully,
to put these thoughts on paper, harness them
the real to tell from dreaming.
Not so well, when we stop to think!

IT'S AN EFFORT TO COMMUNICATE

Thoughts clothed in vibrant words,
To pass forth an inclination.
O'energy bursting out in sound!
But in quandary we express (and do expire),
When desire dies without a breath
Or a breath dies without desire.
We must evermore fill the vacuum,
Horror not the thought, nor the word, but the void.
Dress the thought in undulating sense tones.
We know it's an effort to communicate.
But the deaf do crave for sound
And the world awaits a message.

SOMETHING TO BELIEVE IN

Why are we deluded?
with beliefs we don't know,
why we believe in them?
Why do our hearts love
with a love we don't know,
where that love has come from?
Why do the clouds romp free,
rivers flow to the seas?
Children must grow to love,
believe as we must,
all the things around them?
Love without believing
believe without loving?
Before we die we must
all believe we have loved,
all believe we are loved!

IT'S LOVE THAT CARES

Who is it said, I don't care?
Has thrown stones with words
hard as any hand can.
They've said to every child:
Don't learn to walk, do not run,
just sit there and weaken.

They've said:
Let the volcanoes erupt, rivers dry,
stars fall from the sky.
Let children grub slums day on,
bellies nights with hunger growl!
In effect, they've said, we don't care,
if, tomorrow the world ends foul.

But there are those who care:
Care if the rain falls and the sun shines;
care if fruit trees bear fruits to share;
every child learns to walk, run and talk,
read, and sum, one from two is one.

Time immemorial mothers cared,
heaved full breasts the young to feed.
For them, we wouldn't enjoy singing
birds at the break of day we see,
the painted clouds as the sunsets.

Thankful we must be for:
A miracle ingredient in the air,
it's love, hearts it fills to core.
It lets:

Winds carry pollen to blossoms
we adore,
birds with twigs nests build;
turtles sands dig, lay eggs
miles in.
Peacock's fans of color
charm everyone. Hear
The humming of waterfalls,
murmuring brooks running:
It's love that cares!

LOVE, HOPE AND FAITH

When we hate what we love
And love what we hate;
Fear what we desire
And desire what we fear,
We are ambiguous and inconsiderate.

This we must learn to separate:

Hate and fear is a pair
That goes together down
To the gates of hell.

Love and desire is a pair
That goes together up
To the gates of heaven.

The problem is to distinguish
And separate them.

Who would want to live,
Forever in fear of hell?
Forever hate instead of love!

There're a few more things
The obstinate ignore:

The pair of hope and faith.

Hope is the fountain
From which faith springs,
Without love, hope and faith

Life we could not tolerate.
We would be ambiguous and inconsiderate.

Unconscionable to the neighbors we would be,
We must love and desire without fear and hate!

DON'T JUDGE A BOOK BY ITS COVER

Why we all judge a book by its cover,
As we do our neighbors to no end?
We've lost tolerance in divine books sent.
Judgments become assumed reality
To defend. Never the book to the end
Read. Ever the neighbors befriend!
A life of superficiality lived;
We don't seek the knowledge of things to know,
We shouldn't pass judgment on things we don't know!
The book of life, is the book we should read,
Borrow it from your neighbor this weekend.
To make a friend share the knowledge you've read;
The pages from books can make you best friends!

DINGBATS

Do you "Stop" to think?
Or you "Dash" thru life?
This is a "●" stop,
This is a "▬" dash.
They control your life.
They're used also for
Morse code of dots and dashes,
To send secret messages.
These are ◢↕▶◀↕▲ dingbats,
They just fool around.
The small and different
Are the most significant!
When you express a thought,
At the end you stop "●",
To break away you use a dash "▬"
Don't use Morse code anymore,
To confuse the dingbats. ◢↕▶◀↕▲
If you don't "STOP"
The world will crash!

THE BEAUTY OF THE WILD FLOWER

Hindsight can't help the nearsighted!
We aren't static beings fixed finitely
In time, but strings of energy
Space ascertained, expansively.

My imagination tires not
Conjuring, Freedom many ways,
Like flower hopping honeybees,
Or as restless waves of the seas!

In the sun my reason never fades,
Searching the shores for love I wade,
The love lost in premature affections,
As footprints of hope the waves erode.

In hindsight now I do reflect,
Wondering of the many wrecks
Reaching shorelines in squared off space—
Life is an undetermined race.

I lift my head the sun to see.
Faith I fear, love, hope I endear.
I envy the search of the bee,
The beauty of the wild flower!

MAKING WEAPONS

Man has much to lament
No need to count,
No need to count his joys,
Jubilations,
Countless accomplishments
Through space and time.
He discovered the clouds,
The bugs in swamps.
The smoke and heat of fire.
How to keep warm
In the winter nights and storms.
Berries to pick,
Deer's roast in pits,
Fires he hands lit.
How to crush the hardest rocks,
The nooks to hide.
Swim and fish the widest rivers.
These are his joys.
To survive he climbed the clouds,
Left behind the swamps,
Climbed the highest mountains.
Sitting so high,
He's closer to the skies,
Making weapons!

DICIPLES OF WAR

In my mind thoughts revolving,
Never resolving,
Thoughts of Philosophy.
Great Greek warriors of words,
Socrates, Plato, Aristotle.
See them in sandals, walking, talking,
Flinging robes as to the wind, over their shoulder,
Opening the University.
History making. Whispers of the soul;
Ethos through history. Talk of souls and wars.
Many kinds of souls, many kinds of wars.
Consoling loneliness of the mind, lights in the dark.
We see their shadows against the walls,
Looking for a door, they know, keeps knocking.
No one answers; the slaves say, "The masters
Are out to war." The words are lost. The soul!
With swords on green swards we are out to war!
Words are words, without meaning. They become swords.
Philosophy? We are disciples of war!

POLITICAL MISCHIF

From A Humanistic standing,
All my longings I have explored.
The Renascence as a guide I took—
From Dante to Machiavelli.

Who haven't between the lines read?
Missed the thread leading to a trend:

Neo-Platonism has lead
To Neo-conservatism,
From this political mischief
War to Saddam descends!

We can with might, intimidate,
Never sure why, we dominate!
Sneaky, preeminently we kill

Deluded with grandeur we will,
The world round policemen become,
The weak and weary instill:
Our faith, our views, against their will!

Friendship we cannot cultivate,
Hearts with fear fill—the mind of men!

HISTORY'S CURSE

Medals of Honor cross the grave
As marks of youthful soldiers brave
Die a death not of their will.
But by hearts with hatred instilled—
That's the enemy deep within!

A tomb casts a shallow shadow,
From every angle of the day.
Who can retell in any way,
The color or the depth of an arrow?
Arrows are to kill, not to persuade.

Slingshots kill giant's everyday,
Tyranny cannot have its way.
Armies do not fight for freedom,
It's the hearts throbbing for the sky!

Armies of hatred do fight,
Nor, ignorance sees the light.
Loves might cannot be
Conquered by night—
Justice, never knows which side to take,

Let the rivers flow freely from
Heights of mountains to ocean tides.
It is we, who the currents guide,
And divert love darts in errands sent.
Change history's curse, or fast repent!

THE TERROR IN YOUR HEART

The question I have for you,
Are you the one, who tends to the gardens?
Who sweeps the debris form nuclear explosions,
Who from starvation death clears the stench?
And wipes the tears from all the refugees you see?

I ask these questions as I stop and say hello
But you don't take the time and answer them.
Are you blind from the last explosions?
From high jacked planes over the high seas?
What other terror can you be thinking of,
To frighten a life of heaven out of me?

What in your heart troubles you, which
Expressed in hatred destroys you and me?
God is the only one, who the world has made,
Only He can destroy it, if and when He wills.
The terror in your heart is the terror you impart!
All beasts of the jungle terrorize it isn't smart.

To God suicide is not a ladder to heaven,
But a hangman's rope down to hell.
Destroy the two towers pointing to heaven,
But you cannot destroy the hearts of men!
Mothers' love for sons you've stolen from them.

Men who love the freedom God has given them,
Freedom wider than all the walls of your hell.
Have you lost the love God has given you?
To enjoy on earth and beyond the grave!

Why from heaven's grace you have fallen,
From the mores, heaven, the values of civilized men?

What makes you so brave, you think
You're mightier than He, his decrees destroy?
The love of earth, fellowmen, and heaven He gave.
Evil thoughts strangle your heart, your mind depraved.
Who are you to destroy what God has made?

God will not a reward have for you in heaven,
God wills not rewards for those against His will,
The minds and hearts of children hatred spoiled,

Their freedom to laughter, the lives you've taken,
And His work on earth and heaven, destroyed,
With bombs strapped to sacred temples He's made.

CONSCIENTIOUS OBJECTORS

There is a fine line between defense and offense
And a wide divide between war and peace.
Overstepping the fine line often starts a war,
Which makes the wide divide to Peace wider.

Irony is, free societies choosing not
To fight offensive enemies will find
They aren't free for long. Conscientious objectors
Will not have their free conscience. Their pride derides!

There is one thing our long tradition of wars
Should teach us all, no one is a vector.
War is a catch twenty-two of self-destruction.
The times we are being the victors, we are victims.

Wars are un-edifying to man, woman and child,
Medals chest-bearing generals are not
For long glorified. No lasting glory lasts where enemies
Lurk. Sorrow to lose limb, life and liberty.

It's less edifying to do the will of tyrants.
In the name of liberty and freedom,
We must fight. Human dignity we cannot lose,
Undignified wars fight for dignity.

Can a cause become greater than its destruction?
A moral question must answer itself,
The cause be human dignity and liberty,
Morality is immortality!

To conscientious objectors, we do not object,
It's not a matter of conscience alone,
All for freedom and human dignity must fight:
It's the instinct to war we all must fight!

STOP THE WARRING

Headlong thundering down the trail,
The March rages on to enemy's unseen.
They, with all their might, not this war win.
Who this fight started through eternity?
Angels fallen should be trampled on.
Decrees of fate on sheepskin hastily written
Has no meaning to the blind, but to history.
Peace was smitten as with invisible ink written.
Timid fear cannot in the bosom of valor hide.
Justice lost in the recesses of evil minds
Can't be recovered in careless hearts.
Love was never found where it wasn't planted.
Nor in those who rage over life's dead end.
The successive rise and fall of wars, ever failed,
Hasn't mellowed the hearts of men.
Sounds deafen the ears; Sights blind the eyes;
The tanks' rolling crushes the soul.
What folly grips us to loose reason?
What despair can be greater, than to lose life,
When it's the only one given.
The enemy is not who we fight, it's why we fight:
It is the sinister uncontrolled urge to wield
Power over the unfortunate.
The wage of war cannot repay for one life lost,
Nor, faith in humanity.
Damn to hell those who start, and can't stop warring!
The anger expressed, supersedes compassion—
There is no justice but to save lives.

IS IT TOO LATE

No one wants to die by the hands
of another nor by his hand
when the purpose is not so clear,
or no purpose at all, declared.
Does anyone really want to die?
Die we must, but not by a shot,
ravages of war raging death,
besides the stars humans dying;
or from the time we lived in caves.
We recognize not the souls killed,
nor ours when the tides do turn.
In the rage of fury hands lift,
striking and striking without purpose,
or design, perhaps an impulse
or, is it an instinct to kill?
We hide behind the rocks of time
in the nights' shadow of the moon
we stalk and strike, and strike again,
not knowing why we strike this blow
killing someone we do not know.
We see the blood and rushing flow
a beating heart tells us it's wrong,
something is wrong, is it too late?

WHY SHOULD YOU MARRY ME

Your old time notions of love,
Does not jibe
With my liberalized views of life,
Or with my evolving social theories.
You believe in natural love,
And I in contraception.
I believe that women have a right
To their bodies,
You believe that God does.
You are a conservative who doesn't play
And I a liberal who believes in foreplay.
When you debate with me about ideas,
Which side do you take?
I am pragmatic, somewhat empirical,
You are dogmatic, very sentimental.
If we are so fundamentally incompatible,
Why should you marry me?
We debate about religion and politics,
War and Peace. The four big ones.
You hate to talk about them.
Can we help our children understand?
Why with all our religion, we have wars?
Can we reconcile for them,
Why Politics does not bring peace?
It's time we seek some compatibility!
If not for us, at least for them!

THE SCENT THE FEMALE GIVES

As I sat myself, contemplating,
My life if you will,
I came upon this surprise.
I am made up of organ systems
Of many hues.
Forget about symmetry, they are
Of various sizes.
Looking farther on I saw they were
Just of tissues made,
Miles on miles of them.
Some so delicate and transparent
The sun could see through them.
They were of course composed of
Molecules with funny names and
Dubious weights.
But forget about all this,
For after all:
We are only trillions of atoms
Swirling through imagined space
All hopelessly, eternally racing,
Infinitely, without beginning or end.

I sat there wondering is this all I am?
Then these thoughts occurred to me:

Why do men find delight in
Women's breasts
Forgetting their utility?
Why do women admire a man's
Bare chest
Forgetting its strength?

Why do children snuggle under
Their mother's arms
Seeking love?
Why do other species follow
The scent the female gives and
Only of its kind?
Why do humans arouse each other
With anger and hatred, and do give
Strong love?
In spite of this, do kill!

IT'S TEMPORARY

The contemporary
Is exemplary
But temporary,
Like a cloud roaming around
Not too long in the sky,
Or perhaps, not knowing
Exactly where to go.
Conformity is an agreement
With things we like,
Not because others say we should.
The moronic adhere to
The contemporary,
In which we find contempt.
The contingent is neither
Implicit nor simplistic.
The contentious are
The worst kind, they make
Us feel inadequate.
Thank the heavens our
Contemporary leaders
Are not continuous.

MAKERS OF HISTORY

We are all makers of history,
And all that history has made.
We've left our footprints in the dust
On the moon. And the moon by the hand
Guides us through the eternal darkness of the night.

Moon hopping is the first hopping we've made in space,
We've made it seem so simple,
Others quickly followed the chase,
This race will be hard to win.
For space is such an open place,
No winning post can be seen.

We will be making many trips,
And hopefully will be able to return
Home again on earth to God and to fame.

We have explored the North and South poles,
Many have been lost in the snow,
And the ice has frozen our very souls.
But the spirit that climbs frozen mountains,
And flies the open skies,
Is a spirit that never dies?

II

We have gone to the bottom of the ocean,
Scuba dove in shark infested seas,
Found our way in fathomless blue holes,
Got carried away by currents, lost in underwater caves,
Ferocious animals tamed,

With gunshot, arrows and flint stones.

But there is one animal we haven't tamed,
That animal is: The uncontrolled human mind.
One mountain we haven't climbed,
That mountain is: A heart of stone.
A space we haven't explored,
That space is: The depth of the soul.
We are all makers of history,
And all that history has made.

O! THIS DEMOCRATIC LONGING

To name a name is not to tell a lie.
Where the abundant land meets the roving sky,
One Plum only will fill a Farmer's hand.
One rock will build a home, one rain filled cloud
Will suffice to fill the pond—wet every parched
Tongue!
A child's jubilant face will greet the sky—saying,
"Thank you sky".
You ask where? To tell you when, to tell
You why!
To name a name, you say, is to name a name and to
Tell a lie.
You skeptic friend turned enemy, broke my divining
Rod.

II

On my window I left a note of anxiety.
The winds caught the jest of my grief—
The leaves of many seasons were falling,
And many-colored birds are still flying.
But where was my note to the world?
The secret message to be spoken
Was to look for a friend.
All doors must be called upon,
No heart must be left unturned.
The secret sigh must be a shout—
Our National Anthem must be a smile.
O! This Democratic longing to reach
Every red bird.
Pull the iron curtain down, and let

The sun shine in.
Build a balcony in place of a wall!
Let your maidens receive a song
From the American troubadour.
A friend is not a friend unless he makes
A friend.

III

Now the walls at last are down,
But Democracy is nowhere to be found:
Still the greedy pumps of fuel a' grinding,
In foreign bloody grains of sands a' standing.
But how do we get a much-needed fill?
Without friendship fainting, on knees begging,
Or God forbid, by slander we steal!
Is aggression fair to export still,
The wilted flower of Democracy?
Nor can we preempt, without being preempted!

IV

On the blue-rim horizon of a New Frontier,
When the forests are cleared,
And the prairies are crossed,
When the pioneers of space have won the race.
When the flag of every star is the flag of stars,
We'll see engraved the sun with new Democracy.
One triumph upon another heralds a new era,
And every glory shared with the enemy within.
The cold war was fought on neutral ground,
But it was won by the daring of the new frontier,
The new frontier of a world opened mind.

JEFFERSON TOOK THE CARE TO WRITE

If my mind you shackle in bondage,
You might as well my body enslave.
Whatever choice of names it is called,
With insidious thought to chain my mind.

Your misdeeds are greater than my crime,
A reprobate of society,
Your highfalutin words say I am,
When you're stealing the faith I have.

Don't gag my freedom of religion,
With it confuse my freedom of speech.
The separation of law from creed,
Which Jefferson took the care to write.

This was not easy it took some fight
To preserve the sacredness of both,
For us to prosper as a Nation,
The separation of the state from church.

We must hold this ideology, which is high,
Everyone keeps his right to believe,
Everyone his choice of government,
Without prejudice or bigotry.

Freely worship your option of faith,
Freedom to vote politically
This the constitution says is right,
Respect we all must this sacred trust!

This was intellectual achievement,
Not ostracism blind fate guides,
Holding the courage of conviction
From ignorance and superstition!

THE INVENTION OF A NATION

I am an inventor!
I invent concepts and philosophies.
From these I invent religions, governments and civil liberties,
War and Peace, even a few Kings and a Pope or two.
Some are just catchy gadgets like Fascism or Communism.
Some are very destructive as fanaticism, or libertarianism
Unrestrained.
At last, more by design, not serendipitously,
I invented a self-perpetuating nation,
With the concepts and principles of Democracy.
If you doubt what I am saying ask Tocqueville,
Who came from France himself to see,
How this experiment for freedom works, called Democracy!
He thought he, or countries might benefit from this
discovery.
And in spite of all its ups and downs,
This nation has survived as the home of liberty;
It has survived Civil War, political corruption and religious
dissention,
The terror of hatred of those who our freedom envies.
I didn't only invent a nation,
But a people, a special kind of people, called Americans!
Give character and shape to a new personality,
Give character and shape to humanity.
The design of this invention is the Bill of Rights,
The guarantee of everyone's civil liberties,
The patent of this nation is protected by a Constitution,
Which none should try to steal, or tamper with;
The vision of this constitution is the ideal of highest polity.
It says:

That everyone has a right to freedom, happiness and
property;
That privacy is fundamental to liberty;
Freedom of speech is a right, not a license, to abuse our
neighbors.
It forbids making any law, "Respecting the establishment" of
religion,
Or, "prohibiting the free exercise" of religious beliefs.
This distinction makes this nation great, this we should
understand.
Many misunderstood the invention of this democratic nation,
Tried hard to destroy it,
Even those who from it, the most would benefit!

II

Let's make a few observations,
As Tocqueville did, about this nation,
It's not as perfect a system, as we would like it to be.
It's only as perfect as "we the people" can make it.
Sometimes we make landmark decisions,
Which shake the roots of its very foundation?
We forget to honor and respect the individual,
A fundamental principle we cannot lose sight of.
The abuse of liberty is not a constitution or civil right.
When we legislate values, we may commit a moral wrong,
But who decides what a moral wrong is?
When you make my values wrong,
We have a political and moral conflict.
When the majority is in, the minority
Suffers the tyranny of their whims—
In a Democracy who protects the rights of the minority?
The righteous may not always be right,
The wrong may sometime be right,
It depends where we are coming from—

Justice is hard to define!
We must respect the privacy, and the religion of others,
Before we impose, or legislate about them,
Legality from principles must come.
Principles are not by legality tested,
But the legal must by principles be made.
In legal minds interpretations of the constitution rest,
But how legal and just are these minds?
"We the people" must always decide.

WITH FREEDOM RIDE

I walk the street with pride
Displaying dignity.
Knowing where freedom rides
Not in gold lined coaches
Of old dignitaries
Who barely glanced at me
Standing in cotton fields.
Popes of antiquity
In bullet proof limos
Didn't stop to bless me
Nor help my liberty
When chained I rowed the ship
Of Rome to war and kill
Not a free man but slave
Or cowered in slave ships
As chattel to be sold.
How can man against man
With pride humans enslave?
Human rights none can give.
All are born to be free
Ride in buses' front seat
Ancestors denied.
They ride with us in pride.
There is joy in freedom
Quenching my thirst in a
Five and ten cents store.
None can give liberty
My human dignity
The only fight I fight
To defend liberty!

WHOSE AMERICA

America is a dream I have,
An idea ever dwelling within me:
The idea of being an American!
What it means to be an American,
Is an idea for all eternity!

A generation of Europeans and other
Countries too, coming to find freedom,
Forming settlements and communities,
In common law of equality to uphold.
Who's America? My America!

This dream I dreamed and fought for
No one dares to take away from me.
Forging the prairie, mountain climbing
I am an American from North to South.
Where were you when rough seas I rode?

Cramped in ship holes only the sky to see,
You must pay the price I paid for liberty;
The British fought, the Spaniards and the French.
Risked signing for independence, the constitution,
In civil war sided with Lincoln the slaves to free?

If you want to live like me, with me
I'll neighborly open my doors legally,
We'll enjoy peace, freedom and liberty.
Don't on the streets display flags defiantly,
Enough the flag of the USA for you and me!

Immigrants we all are, who come

To form a country in civil liberty.
In union share the dream of America,
Roots to form, our children live free;
Knowing the rock of liberty is honesty!

LET US PRESERVE THIS NATION

Why do you have a different idea of human nature than I
have?
How can you liberally call me a conservative, and I
conservative
That I am, call the ideas you have liberal? What do we really
want?
Why are my lies, lies, and your lies nothing but the truth?
Don't we want the same things? The safety of our nation!
Want to defend our nation and live by and uphold the
constitution?
Put a gate at the border to stop illegal trafficking, stop bombs
And drugs from coming in? Let the legal voters speak their
mind,
Let them have prosperity and retire comfortably? Taxed
evenly!
Exchange goods they make for the ones they want, without a
deficit!
Balance the economy, create jobs, give charity, and be
admired
As the cradle democracy. Liberal you say you are and
conservative
You say I am, we shouldn't let differences destroy this nation!
Can we stop the fury of lying and the deceit of deceiving,
Can we bury the hatchet; bring our solders back marching,
Not in coffins!

THANKFUL TO SPEAK OUR MINDS

In the background of our minds,
Where reminiscing seems to start,
There are galleries of pictures,
From childhood, to high school,
And weddings. None of funerals.
We don't celebrate funerals. Why?
No one takes pictures at a funeral.
We don't see family albums with pictures
Of dead love, only of the weddings.
Death should be as comforting to
The living as to the dead. On many
Occasions it should be cause of celebration,
If peace it brings after much suffering.
We are infatuated with high virtue,
Which we think is the only joy.
Holy matrimony can be agonizing to endure.
Vague ideas in our minds difficult to define.
There is also something hypocritical
About all those wedding pictures.
We think they are unifying,
But not when some beloved is dying.
Sometimes it's the mind that tricks us,
Because we think we know it all.
We think we have a thought of our own,
When the thoughts of others we are repeating.
This is not hypothetical we've done it
From day one. This is why we think
Our virtues are more virtuous than all.
When we illustrate a point, we do it
With contempt, forget about clarity,
It's the point we want to make, that's important!

We try to enunciate the thoughts in our minds,
But we don't pronounce them too well,
Sometime they sputter anger and disappointment,
Sometimes they come with different accents,
Like some cheap imported wine. It intoxicates,
But it also gives us a hangover of a lifetime.
There are many more faded pictures
In the back of our minds, they are hard to see,
We are thankful we can speak our minds!

I WANT TO SING ABOUT FREEDOM

I want to sing about freedom, would you sing along with me?
What does freedom mean to a free society
When society is gag-bound by terrorist bombs?
Terrorism we must know comes in many forms not only
from foreign lands.

What did the Bill of Rights mean to Lee fighting at
Gettysburg,
Without talking to Lincoln about slavery and liberty?
The birth of freedom has its agonies as the death of Socrates
did.
What does that mean to religion, and what religion says
To democracy about the decline of morality?
Gibbon knew all about the fall and decline of Rome, did he
know
What Jesus said to Paul? Did he say: go build churches to
save the world?
The question we must ponder, from what is humanity to be
saved?
If it is to be saved, it's from its own destructive tendency.
What freedom does a church provide when we need a pass to
enter
And we are restrained from leaving freely, if we will. Isn't this
why Luther led the Protestant Reformation? It wasn't only
him: Machiavelli questioned the Divine Right of Popes and
Kings—in Civil Disobedience who is being disobeyed? Must
we have a plan
When we must fight for social change, for the freedom of
every man?
Shall we follow Kant, letting the rightness of freedom dictate
its course of action?

What freedom lessons can we learn from Alexander the
Great? What hope!
Did he help Jefferson, Adams and Madison with the
Declaration of Independence?
The French revolution was a failure, a disgrace to the cause of
free men.
What tradition tells us about freedom, when Hitler overran
Poland?
No one seems to care, until Pearl Harbor was bombed by
Japan, and then it was almost late. Roosevelt and Churchill
knew the danger, and the enemies of freedom they fought.
Today there are as many enemies of freedom as history has
ever known.
Freedom as a human idea is taking too long to root in our
hearts,
Where are the great men we can depend on, to defend
freedom to the bone?
The human heart longs for that freedom without complaint,
That can follow the dictates of its autonomy,
Uncoerced by any authority, rather than its own restraint:
That's ontological freedom beyond selfishness, or ideology.
Let's sing as loud as we can about freedom and do our part!

I want to sing about freedom:
When we are mentally, emotionally and physically free—
Freed from history's lies, ignorance, greed and hatred—
We'll be flying with seagulls beyond the seas.

I want to sing about freedom:
When wrongs are made right and no evil we see—
Freed from political oppression, economic slavery and
bigotry—
We'll be flying with seagulls beyond the seas!

Section 2

THE OTHER SIDE OF DEFENSE

THE OTHER SIDE OF DEFENSE

A cat rolling to a stall,
Almost stopped—he heard the bark of a dog,
Breaking his sense of peace.

The cat leaped on a fence,
In defiance to trace the sound—
The jump was very strained—
Defense takes much resolution!

But the dog was on a leash,
The cat was unrestrained.
Yet the cat his balance kept,
Precariously on top of the fence.

His curiosity barely satisfied,
He knew the threat on the fence,
The other side of the defense.

His anxiety was flares of instinctive drives.
Did he had the strength to lift his entity
Out of the predicament, to save his identity?

It takes courage to open the cognitive
Floodgate to affirm our identity!

The dog took no offence
To the scary cat on defense.

THE FLARES AROUND AND AROUND

THE SUN

Delight of Minerva woman of god.
Sunlight shining light of fire,
Sparkle flickering rose red.

She pricked her ivory finger as
An intrusion to her delightful
Blood squeezed by drops gleaming.

O night of love when the moon
Condones this one impulse to give,
And the elusiveness of the pulse
Beating upon the bare chest of men.

The pressure was as a bow on
Harmony's strings drawn to cord
To create the symphony of woman,
From the tips of her toes and the
Strands of her hair wind blown.

Who knows what the mystery
Will fulfill when the love hunger
Flares around and around the sun,
After the moon has gone down.

Woman by Adam prayed for—
Her advances he did not reject,
Nor the throb of the undying passion.
They beheld each other instantly
In the one furtive cosmic impulse!

Love is of the emotions,
Reason is of the intellect—
Compassion the fruit of their holy bed.
The thorn-pricked hand of reason drips
Blood congealing, no sigh—now feeling—
Only wisdom's silence reeling!

Did Adam spend the night to a harlot wed,
And engendered the dialectical materialist?
O mystery of man's beginning and melodramatic end.
The tyranny of the mind as much enslaves,
As the deceptive dictates of the passions.
Man alas, is not alone; and the world
Someday in eternity be gone—
With all our pomp, with all our glory!

OUR SOULS WE'VE SMASHED

The body standing alone
Disavows me.
Free from the horrors of pain,
Free from the joys of pleasure,
Dislodged from the sense of "I"
The trillions of cells multiply and die.
Hand in hand the ego they displace.
They don't need me,
To complete their mission.
With moral right they fight
To follow their written codes DNA.
They know the "I" is thief, a traitor,
Who deceives to usurp all the powers of nature,
To rule as king, over heaven and hell.
They know the ego is a thing of this world.
When the cells themselves finally dissolve,
The ego doesn't follow beyond the grave.

II

When we come of age we think we are smart.
At least our children think they know it all.
(everyone thinks his / her children are beauty incarnate,
and "bright" as hell.)
We all think we speak poetry,
When we write that biographical novel,
When we read Theology aloud for all to hear,
Even if it's all above their heads—we don't care
What faith they hail from—faith or no faith.

When we come of age we try to find the Self

Which we haven't lost. An Ephemeral Winged Self,
Which only in the imagination, of the deranged exists.
Sometimes we think we see halos round our heads
But we see sharp red devil's horns instead,
Mostly all on our neighbor's foreheads.

We sail on ships we build, and swim to the bottom of the
sea
We fly between the clouds in man-made crafts, and rocket
Far and wide beyond the skies, beyond layers of
stratosphere!
We've picked a hole in matter, through and through, at last.
Alas! And we finally lost the atom somewhere.
We see radiant mushroom clouds everywhere.
Perhaps it's our souls we've smashed?

We've looked high and far and wide,
We have never found the spark behind the sun,
Where we think the Self could hide.
We speak poetry, write Theology, and that
Never ending novel about ourselves, lost in space,
But we do not find between the lines a Self,
Neither our deceived, elusive souls!

IN WONDER DREAM

When we look at the beauty of the rose in wonder,
We see how mysteries the petals weave, one by one,
Miraculously, the air with delicate scents is under.
With prickles strewn, the stems from which they grow;
Sustains varied forms, rare marvels, for us to know.
But if with careless hands these stems we tightly grasp,
Blood from our fingers to earth will drop and clasp,
Drop by drop, as petals one by one, in the sun will gleam.
Every flower the secret of life contains—every sunbeam.
May we never awake, never, from this sweet sweet dream!

HE SWEPT THE FALLEN STARS IN THE CREVICES OF TIME

The lone figure of a man,
Is a question mark beckoning
Everyone to pause before his statue.
The question is—who was first?
He or the echo of color breathing
Upon the cooling cinders an entity?

He swept the fallen stars
In the crevices of time; to
Spread love's warm blanket
Where the egg was to hatch on stone.
He gave emotion to the event; now,
Who can disentangle him from the serpent's hug?
Forgiven should be his first dare,
And we tend with parental care
Every speck of holy dirt!

WHERE CONDORS FLY

No one has seen the Grand Canyon,
As the Condors do!
Specula fete of nature for eons displayed,
Wingspan to wingspan the Condors surveyed.
Looking into nature's bosom through the windows of time.
Depth, length and width of every stone merging to shrines:
A miraculous panorama of wonder to extol,
Drawing our breath out into a sigh. A cry!
Carried away by dimensions of history, evolution roll,
Hard to understand, how it all began.
Wondering night after night how they see in the dark,
See what we cannot see, seen what we haven't seen.
Knowing histories of native tribes keen;
Having made of caves a home, a landmark,
And worship the earth more than the sky.
We wonder how they learned to make nests on peaks,
On cliffs to lay their eggs. Their instincts comply.
How they feed their young and teach them to fly,
Avoiding nooks and crevices where predators hide,
Navigating through the winds, and mysteries of mystery,
They choose to call their home, spread their young wings to
glide.
Yes, the marriage of the Condors, and the Canyons
Never fail to incite emotions deeper that we can endure.
They gracefully display their beauty for us to behold,
But never expose the romance, the secret bond of their
love.
One of the many secrets Nature from us withholds.
Never in all eternity for us to secure!

THE RED OAKS OF CLIFORNIA

Assist creation with fruitful thoughts.
And do more to help. Do your part.
The lasting things created with my hands,
Sweat, work, highways and bridges, the imagines from my
mind
That guides. Never suffice.
But it is pleasant also, sitting under the shade of trees,
Walking, swimming; and the dream to fly.
I respect the birds, making room for the grass,
The weeds to grow. Respect the shadows the sun casts;
The boys with hoops playing; the ones by the side ditch
digging,
And the man on the striding, gleaming horse.
Why do we procrastinate in front of beauty? Don't
question mystery!
I am confused. I tend to forget the things around from
Which I am formed, they make me what I am.
A shining stone skimming over a lake. A frog upon a Water
Lilly
Croaking songs for other frogs to hear, for them to
understand.
We are blind because we do not think. There is so much
To appreciate!
Sit under the shade of a thousand year Red Oak,
Meditate: World attitudes that dominate.
Growing from different soil. People's whims.
Not from the monks shaven head,.
Walking slowly, counting steps. Watching where they tread,
Their robes flowing ocher red.
We must contemplate the little flower
Blooming by the crag, against all odds.
Respect, admire the magnificent, solemn Red Oak,

Standing silent. Enduring!
Nature's Cathedrals celebrating life:
The Red Oaks of California!

THE FLOWER AND THE BEE

I stepped upon a lily, frightened,
To the rose and the bee she called:
"Did you resent the intrusion?"
She asked, with carrying voice for all.

Their sorrow I cannot retake.
How can I apologize for
My thoughtless action to the trees—
Trespass to the ecology?

It's not the indiscriminate
Falling of trees only deplored,
But the shameless extinction of
Humming birds and ladybugs low!

When in wonder birds we all see,
Winging across a rising sun,
And the clouds harmful rays shading,
We sense, it's the way it should be.

I must see where I ruthless step,
Carefully must think what I do:
I may never again see love,
As have the flower for the bee!

II

The rhythm of the Universe sustains,
The harmony of the ecology!
This miracle easy we can destroy
With one thought, one bad deed to beast and man!

THE MYSTRY OF THE ROSE

When my heart with a sigh up heaves, it lights desire in me,
as hot as coal,
To transcend the beauty of the rose my senses apprehend.
The mysteries of her
Sweet perfume inhaled, are mists of ethereal air whiffed by
my free and roaming soul!

If beauty I can transcend, I wonder where it begins, and will
surely end.
Is it all an illusion, the mountains and the valleys I see, the
rivers flow?
When I awake in the morning, my memory brings to me
vistas of the days before.

I, the beauty of the rose cannot forget, a hanging cloud,
sweet aroma
In the air! My beginning or my ends I cannot foretell, break
the sweet spell.
Why we the gods do speak, in language we do not
understand, not a grain of sand?

O! Mystery of life projected, high and low, entrapped my
soul with love and joy
evermore!
I must live as one with the nature of all I have seen—the
mystery of the rose!
They and I are one with ocean waves breaking, night and
day, upon the sands shore.

Histories made, histories forgotten, I am here to stay—here
to stay forevermore!

I must not my soul to hell surrender, or to fairylands all
misbegotten,
My mind with cults old or new, with folklore superstition—
all with mischief rotten!

The philosopher I will befriend. The helpless children, the
old, infirm, defend.
I will not pretend and with injustice side, nor with deceit,
white lies or black, slide
On the priestly kind I cannot depend, nor offence, let them
mad with angels end!

THE ROSES IN EDEN

When I see the sight of your body,
I have seen the sculptors' art full form;
When I hear the sound of your voice,
I have heard the greatest symphony of all;
When I smell the fragrance of your hair,
I have inhaled the roses in Eden before the fall;
When I savor the taste of your lips,
I have been kissed by all the angels in heaven;
When my senses are touched by your soul,
Its radiance fuses yours to mine.
When life we share it's sacramental wine
From the rarest grapes ever grown.
Love is the bread we break,
To feed our empty hearts.
I am a poor mortal condemned to die,
Be merciful, O! Immortality!

REFLECTIONS NOTHING MORE

Our thoughts and all we fancy reflections are
From the mirror of our imagination.
Flying wings of unspoken histories
Evil proclaiming in angel form
Anticipating the division of right from wrong.
Every thought for traces searching
Between the cracks of time, ghosts
Before the dawn of their beginning.
They see streaks of lightening conceiving,
Pregnant with the speed of light,
Through emptiness traveling before space began.
To unknown destinations chasing
Flairs of fire from the emerging sun.
Surges of fluid "Being" everywhere racing, time.
Expanding to the edges of space, to endless void.
Liquid energy matter forming mountains solidified,
High, escaping quenched from the oceans floor.
Swells of waves and rising tides escorting
Sperm from the heaving bosom of the seas,
Ova piercing on lustful sands to infinity.
Suddenly egresses the cell of life slowly evolving,
Making its way upon the sun baked land
Newly formed by an unknown hand; randomly
It swims, crawls, walks and everywhere flies
Dispersing to the four corners with the wind.
Unfortunately, forthrightly, it becomes man talking,
Asking, unreasonable questions no one
Is supposed to know the answers to.
Arrogance already forming he answers:
Miracle! A miracle we behold nothing more!
He doesn't know, it is thought creates all;
Reflections from his reflections; phantoms

From the mirror of uncompromising imagination.
From a mind as blank as a cloudless sky
Emerges sparks of fire as, from the sun!
Imagination is the weaver of our dreams,
The night conspires, listening patiently
To our stories. No one else listens—no One!

THE SUN A MASTER REFLECTOR IS

The sun a master reflector is
Ambiguous the way it rolls around
It is supposed to shed light on things
And show where the shadows are
Sometimes it creates them to remind us
Where the darkness was (supposed to be)
Sometimes it just stands there solemnly
Like some wise man a smirk on his face
Admired to point of an idol worshipped
Once for a god taken to be above
Maybe just one amongst the other gods
Tripping the sky for place and rank each
Vying for our credulous beliefs (or our lies)
Thirty thousand years ago and recent
We all believe stupid imaginary things
Many such beliefs are mucilage stuck
Some beliefs are ancient monuments
Like pyramids piercing the landscape
Or crevices of time breaking space
Or the other thing we take for treasures
Never the mind freaking in darkness
Counting shadows wondering when how
To avoid the pitfalls they find to hide
Or more to the point they are bogged
Wagons go' west to California
Stuck in the mud gold suppose to be
By its color the sun is gold filled
Treasure is now what we know and more
The gold is in the mind not the mines
The sun and gold mimic one another
Fooled we all are and the wise
The wise stumbles over sun and gold

The sun is like a professor with
A smirk who wants us to believe they
Know it all Standing on a platform
In space to make us seem small children
They think we are professors are admired
Like sacred cows like a secret crush
Of the mind for the mind an illicit
Sensual insidious sexual urge to
Be pregnant with knowledge or to father

Virtue sucks mother's breasts dry of molecules
But perversion is some kind of hatred
Aroused when young minds are inseminated
Raped mental transmissible diseases
Professor can be in black robes flowing
Wearing confused collars backwards bringing
Crosses out the shadows the sun to shine

THE ATOMS OF IMAGINATION

The reflection I see in a mirror
Hides the shadows cast by the bright ceiling light
Behind my right shoulder aching with pain
I do think it's arthritis given from
Marathons ran many times to win fame
My mind is wondering how to break strings
Of thoughts chained to my life without reason
There're so many of them to remember
Many we can forgive but can't forget
Oh I was thinking about the photons
Passing through the mirror leaving shadows behind
Wondering is the mirror a flat wall
Or a wide rip through dimensions of time
When the atoms of my imagination
Hold hands with the atoms of the mirror
From the mirror are reflected images of my images
For all eternity to remember
It's fun to poke holes through time with the mind
It boggles the mind to travel through time
But it's harder to figure the return
When with imagination we all learn
To manifest through the wide rips of time
We'll live in the nine dimensions of space
The ninth heaven will be our domain
Who in his right mind would want to return?
To run marathons again to win fame
We should wonder about the chains of thoughts
Our lives are bound to without reason.

OUR FOIBLES YEARNING

Our foibles yearning for inspiration grabs
flying fantasies moving around in the air.
Ambition concentrated on success overlook
failures. Explosive forms of achievement forge
legends of history pages the future to read.
References to future civilizations,
would be attempts to dodge the blame of negligence
hiding behind curtains of desert storms.

It's histories' choice to give a name not take the blame.
No one really takes the blame for our failures,
hidden behind the rocks of time, buried from sight.
Is it too far in time for us to look at Rome?
Its grandeur and legacy can't be avoided.
Exploits of centurions on chariots thrill us still,
the valor of gladiators and their resolve,
puts faith to shame, and our aspirations in
question. We don't hear the sound of chariots rolling
on cobblestones—The stakes of the Palisades,
and the stench and many horrors of the stockade.

Can we break away from history, its legacy?
Vipers spoke in the senate as in our own.
Human motivation can't be buried in sand.
Thumbing through the encyclopedia of our
Human memory all from volumes A to Z,
much has been forgotten buried with the debris,
much we do remember could just as well have been.
The bad fills hundreds of pages, the good but few.
There are many volumes written of fairytales,
some pretend to be autobiographical,
when in fact they are fictional, egotistical.

So much for our human glory lost in time,
now is the time, a different story we must write.
All the grandeur of Rome lost in the dark ages,
beyond the lights of the renascence be retold.
Rome's the grandfather of our civilization,
a monument of human creativity.

The winds and the thunder of human achievement,
open new wider views beyond the horizons.
Evolution cannot be accelerated,
nor stopped, everything must be according to time.
The code of time can't be cracked, nor space be fractured.
Only in the vault of the human heart can vials
of concentrated love be stored for the future.
Human idiosyncrasies our specialness,
humans we are beyond the heavens and the stars.
Minds must be open to save all humanity!

Section 3

ARE FEELINGS THE SAME

ARE FEELINGS THE SAME

Have you tried to image a feeling?
Whatever it's called, it feels the same.
Feelings have been given many names,
Whatever the name they feel the same.

Since we cannot imagine a feeling,
Can anyone tell from where it comes?
Is it something we give, or given;
Is their meaning only in the name?

Some feelings are called love, some called hate,
Some are, happiness, joy, sadness, grief,
A few more, jealousy and anger.
They have a name, but where do they come from?

Are they the same, only different named?
Feelings regardless the name we give,
Can be destructive, swing our mood,
Guide all thoughts, form our attitudes!

THE PICKET FENCE SHADOW

Doorbells of sensation ringing complex in painted houses,
Awake the memories of pleasure-seeking phantoms.
In the half-open door slides only shadows of the night
By the light of many-faced moons circling slowly,
Glowing, torturing round, making one more go
Around this hypercritical amphioxus fancy!

Silent picket fences striped the well-kept lawns,
Keeping the illusion of concentrated boundary.
If by diminished space love is to be overcome,
The moon's concern to give light may be quenched—
Then ghosts may float 'round the dark embankments,
And the picket fences shall stripe the lawns no more.

And the picket fences shall stripe the lawns no more,
When light shall not reflect only the shadow-man.
Stripes in the dawn of darkness will not glow,
And the shrill welcome-bell shall not be still,
When fences away can be willed—and no,
No more tortured strips of light fenced in!

IF THEY STOP EXPLORING

As I lay prone watching the stars something went wrong,
All night the skies were lit up with flashes of wheeling
Hoops of light from supernovas breaking up the heavens.
My thoughts were caught in all this smashing that went on.
There was a reprieve but it was wantonly only in my mind,
As premonition of things to come that I know very well
Will never come. Were stars exploding only in my head, it's
so
Promiscuous, because there were so many imploding.

Watching primordial atoms of energy keeps me going,
They form loops of intrinsic equations to no end.
I see them mixing gene with gene from one ancestral d.n.a.
I move my head from side to side on the bed searching,
Knowing that if they stopped exploring my world would
end.
Earth makes such a comfortable bed, green grass moist,
so soft and
Springy. Who would want to lie and dream anywhere else?

THE LAUGH'S ON US

We all have conflict with our self-image,
We never see ourselves through other's eyes.
We see a narcissistic picture we carry
In our wallets, as if it were, a portrait of
Someone we love. Some have poor estimation
Of themselves, their self-image deflated
As the currency of third world countries.
It's sometimes taken for counterfeit money
Easy to detect. Others like the deceived
Will not admit their faults . Others try
To impress us with their self-importance
Riding in oversized Limousines, windows down.
It presents so many comic situations
To accent comedy to cosmic proportions.
That's cause to make us pause, glance around.
It's really the unexpected that makes us laugh.
The laughter is usually on us, until the
Image in the mirror talks back to us,
Of course all this is an unexpected turn,
Which exposes how fickle, errant and erratic we are!

A PROMISE OF LOVE

Why to me on my cheeks
you kiss,
While others on their
lips?
Why to me your love denied
and belied,
And you speak of races, and
confuse my gender?
Why pretend to be my love
forever,
If indeed you don't care?
You are my neighbor and I am yours,
born here on earth,
In this tough neighborhood!
We share the nights in the day we fight,
it's not right. Why?
I am lost in city buildings and
blind alleys,
And you don't rescue me.
It is you who brought me from
a foreign land.
You promised me life, love and happiness.
You gave me a ring with the colors of
the rainbow,
And showed me the horizon
brilliant by a rising sun.
But you renege on the promise made of
paradise in a garden.
You told me you were the Builder of Heavens
and I trusted you!
You told me you were the architect of Universes

and I believed you!
You promised to love me now
and forever,
And you have deceived me.
I feel by your kiss betrayed,
but I love you!
You leave me very little choice,
I must love you, or hate you.
I must dare to ask, do you
really care?

O! Despot! You've made me a slave
of Your love.
Hold me in bondage as a
tyrant would;
No one dares, because of you,
to vie for my heart!

A RING NEVER WORN

The bureau of my life
Some antique it is,
Crafted by some craftsman,
No one remembers anymore.

It has many drawers' garments stored,
Never, ever worn before;
Gifts, and a ring long forgotten,
How and why they come to be.

Somewhere there was a stock of
Memories I had hid a long time ago;
There was a bundle of letters
All with foreign stamps on them,

From someone with a golden pen,
Promises of love nothing more:
A heart too far away to get to know—
Letters, a ring from someone, never worn!!

THE COMPROMISE IN A PROMISE

Breaths of hearts sighing,
Waves of potential music.
A silence has been broken,
By the ripples of existence.

Living waves of mysteries widening.
Strange elements making contact
To bring forth the unknown—
Maybe love? Maybe pain? Maybe grief?

Happiness is compromised in a promise,
Which for no rhyme or reason in heaven,
Nor on earth, was ever made!

GUARDIAN ANGELS

I'm reading this poem entitled: "Angels On Earth Flying". It all sounds so evangelical, but at the same time so lyrical, it sings about angels flying, birds winging and the sun peeking with red brilliant eyes. I would think it more appropriate to say, angles floating, birds flying and the sun shining. But of course, I am not poetical. It sets me wondering where the word evangelical came from, is it from angels or Evangeline? Evangeline is a lady I know, who for a living drives Limousines.

She claims she has a guardian angel that rides in the empty seat beside her. She claims this angel guides her; in fact, this angel rides around town beside her, and keeps her accident free. As crazy as this sound, I have no reason to doubt her, but she showed her license accident free. She is very conversant with these sorts of things. She has to be, you have to have a lot of street smarts to drive limousines.

She was trying to explain the difference between Evangelism and Existentialism, but it went right over my head. I guess it's like the difference between birds winging and flying and the sun peeking and shining. One thing she said I understood: Evangelists riding in her limousine to the TV studio to
preach about heaven and hell from the donations tipped her very well.

She said that an evangelist told her, "Keep talking to the angel in the empty seat beside her." He also told her, "Thousands of angels can stand on a pin's head." She said she really believed him and went to Wal-Mart and

bought a whole case of pins. She said, "It was a job related
accident I got converted."

She said she once asked an evangelical if he was her
guardian angel and he answered: "Hell no, I am just a
preacher who
  makes a living preaching." He was dressed like Regis
Philbin,
  and wore Floersheimer shoes, but carried a begging
  bowl as
  St. Francis did.

I have no reason to doubt her, but it's really humorous
  to
picture a thousand angels dancing on a pin's head.
But am
not taking any chances; I wear a safety pin on my lapel.
  I can't stop thinking about evangelism and existentialism.
  I better finish reading this poem it may prove beneficial!

Section 4

MY MISPERCEPTIONS

MY MISPERCEPTIONS

Fearlessly I tread upon the path of life,
Never weary in my tireless search,
To find the one, who would say to me definitely:
"It's I who the beauty of the Lily, of the orchid, made!"

Hopelessly my dreams exceeded my expectations:
Nightmares with malignant, evil spirits filled!
Every turn on the highway of life I take,
Helplessly in the wrong directions has lead.

Breathlessly I have journeyed to lost destinations;
Desperately, I seek a way out my misperceptions!
The guiding hand of the one I seek, should be the one
To guide the child, the wise, the sculptor chisel in hand!

THIS DREAM OF LIFE WE SHARE

Life may be a dream we are having,
Awake! In the West the stars are fading,
The East the morning sun arising;
The mind a fog of blank horizons,
Through which no bird dares to fly.

Until thoughts rise chasing in the sky,
Bringing with them the withered vines
Of our recollection of forgotten lies
And of dreams of dreams we've had.

Life becomes only the memory of life,
A memory of fancy dreaming.
As hard as we try we can't sort
The fantasies from the fads.

Dreaming often becomes nightmares,
In which neighbors we fight day long.
We struggle and shout loud as we can,
For someone reliving this anguish we have.

This dream of life we share,
From which none to awaken care,
Or belie the heavens, the stars dare;
The challenge hectic nightmare brings.

If a dream of life we are dreaming,
What nightmares might be scheming?
Can we depend on the future, be it the sky?
Can we stop dreaming, depending on a lie?

No one by his or her accord seek life,
Few by their accord seek death,
Many in darkness avoids the sun—
To question the stars the days have come!

GENEESIS RETOLD

You've heard the story of creation,
The Genesis opportunity lost.
Paradise to lose for eternity,
To the couple Adam and Eve.

It's said, Eve by a serpent was tempted,
And with Adam shared the apple she stole.
Said, a sin of disobedience it was,
Or, was the hunger for knowledge the cause?
Outcast of Paradise ever become.

In Genesis between the lines the story
Is told of human love for another;
The story is expressed by a gift forbidden,
An apple symbolizing a love beyond
The carnal. A tragedy unfolds—
As love proves stronger than an order.
Genesis obscures the real reason the
Order was given: Knowledge to withhold

Eve with love gave the apple to Adam.
It was no merely speculative binge,
But, the spectacular idea of love
First time felt. A whispered continuum:
We'll have happiness if life we take now,
A consequence of imagination,
A reverberating splash today felt,

When hope-by-hope is led, beyond what's said;
This love we've found is a Quantum leap through
The black hole of our lost souls through time.

It was hard to find our miniscule
Souls, merged with the stellar swirls of space.

When Adam saw Eve his heart went "Big Bang".
The gravity of their hearts revolved around
The relativity of Paradise—
Creation has been hypothetical.
But their love grew to infinity fast,
And vast, to grow planets, starts and galaxies.

Eve said to Adam, it's so good to roam,
Through the Universes thought has made
Of squares of energy too small to see,
And, our reflections in parallel
Universes—a duplicate it seems.

Genesis doesn't tell how our love ends:
Is evolution a contribution?
Which God has made for all eternity?
Are we capitulating to the notion—
Paradise is a garden God has made?

THE GODS WE SERVE

Starting with Greek mythology and perhaps beyond, the story of creation epoch to epoch in many tongues is told. But many hold on to evolution, which with reason they behold. Accepting our evolutionary trend, who can tell how far we may end? We may end as planets in a galaxy. All odds are in favor of this possibility. Many through the ages have turned their backs shunning all responsibility. It's easy to see how we can contribute to this accomplishment. This view lets us see, we have a lot we can do, a lot we have done, as far as we dare to go, a lot more can be done. All the gods from either disposition are on our side for this long journey.

We can sail the skies in golden chariots for all to see, or stay on earth and cultivate the soil. Leave a solid inheritance to our prodigy. It seems we have been here for all eternity in different forms of forms evolved. It really matters not where we came from, only how we evolved, and the direction we decided to go. We know the story of our creation, page by page, in many myths is told; plot on plot is sewn with the threads of our imagination. We can join hands and form gangs with any god we choose. We can become the subject of Zeus or, take flights in space with Apollo, go to bed all night with Aphrodite! Or why not more easily, entrenched become with the gods of Abraham? Or write new testaments. We were driven out of Paradise, dared not look back, for a pillar of salt we might turn. How we take our reflections for gods to adore, or gods who our enemy becomes, our masters, and as slaves demand we serve? In clouds of illusion the deluded hide to rob the innocent and the gullible of hope and pride.

Historically, when cults gain respectability, they design
 to
take control, even the power of Kings they dethrone.
They
disinvest the rights of every man; treason is to deny
the right to reason.
Their perfidies with treachery condemn the human
soul. At least with evolution we leave our lower selves
behind.
What ignorance blinds reason, when reason is blinded
 By destiny? All destinies are man made! Humans are
dynamic
to their own end with power to destroy, or elevate
them.
Newton's law of inertia metaphysically stated: every
 act
brings its own retribution. What quarks of mind allow
 us
to accept the historicism of past cultures without
question? A culture is only important to its own
moment,
and its own end. We must be free to develop by the
dynamism of our needs.
Can we glorify the agonies of the past without an
 Express expense to the future? Intelligence should
 have the
foresight to climb, make flights in space with Apollo,
leaving the slimy rocks behind. See how the sun
shines relatively brighter, from an expanding view in
space! Each epoch designs its own gibberish, speaking
to future generations in a foreign tongue. Those who
pretend to
understand, but pretend to know. Are we to succumb
to such mentality?

THOUGHTS BREAKING THE WALLS OF HELL

Thought breaking the restraints of our minds,

Reason never climbing the ladder of fame
May precipitously fall to hell.
We cannot stand on shifting sands that well.
Roaming from galaxies to galaxies,
Believing we are a special elite group
Privileged to search the skies flying,
To find that special place where it begins.
Where He may dwell in peace that lit the lamp,
That lights the stars and all the other worlds,
Reaching other worlds beyond our own.
We will lose the firm ground on which we stand,
How can we avoid the stars colliding?
Intentions scattered to unwelcome hearts,
Habits are high explosives without care
They will shatter love and hope everywhere.
With technology accelerating,
And sentiments in time being left behind,
No one breaks away from the wall of time.
We believe we are an elite group,
Collateral disasters none avoid.
Avalanches of snow objectives drown,
Can we send rescue teams to outer space?
Our world begins where we are standing,
Space isn't a safe place for the human race.

Mental infectious diseases spreading,
Undermines the most stable feeling,
Authorities reputation questioned.
Insight levels of projected perspectives,
The dreams we should dream insomnia denies.
The control of contagious diseases
Of insidious ideologies is hard,
So being subservient to pushy word storms.
The disturbing fury of our thoughts,
As howling winds must be by force contained,
I will give you my guiding hand to hold
But you must steadily walk,
The walk leading to your dreams fulfilling.
I carry this lofty idea in me
Head all to full with human dignity,
A notion filling my heart few do have.
When we go to bed at night and do rise
Commemorating human dignity,
No greater glory can we humans have.

Imaginative invocations for
Divinely inspired societies,
Prayer's a function offering promises,
Fulfilling many of our social needs,
It should not be used to win wars we fight,
Or historical events influence.
Needs are links to divine intervention,
Generosity of the heart abounds.
Part of my religious charmed sweetness comes
From the air I bread, the breath of life giving,
The other from the magic in your heart.
The wisdom of what I say history comes,
Not from much I know, but what I believe.
Infinity does not stop the crying,
It's the lament of piety in the air.
When angels come what do they appease?

Are they rescuing team's relief to bring?
The determination to find the truth,
That truth by which we all in peace can live,
Shakes the roofs of heaven its gates to open!
I will place my magic charm round your neck,
Guiding you back from all imagined hell!

THE ABSOLUTE A NIGHTMARE

Infinity is indivisible,
Eternity, no beginning, no end!
Mortal that I am,
Would kill for the argument:
"Neither can be known;
The absolute a nightmare!"

When we turn sensations into feelings,
And feelings into emotions, we can
Turn emotions into sentiments,
Which become the building blocks of meaning.
Purpose is to be actors on a stage,
The backdrop of existence but a cage.

Thus we each the dramas of life create!

Climb a cloud upon another,
Bare our chests in rain,
Stripped of our thoughts and feelings
A Self we cannot find:
None for all our pain to care!

The absolute a nightmare,
Infinity illusion,
The eternal nowhere!

Pietistic affections dashed
Against a cosmic wall,
Which, in all reality isn't there—

All delusions…
A quantum void we stand upon.
We all despair!

EXISTANCE BRINGS FORTH SURELY

I know not where I came from,
And I know not where I'll go,
But this conscious being I am,
I didn't make, nor can I make.

We should stop to think of this
At night and the break of day:
The Universe could be just
Projected space awareness!

The dimensions of space are
Mental steps we take in time
To form the sky and the rain,
The earth, to bloom flowers and weeds,

This world, which we think we have
Is an Illusion a magic lantern,
Of aspirations made,
No more than a thought, a shade.

Am I not this consciousness,
Which I think I am alone?
Am I that which I divvy
With and every Human Being?

Whatever Existentially
Shared determined destiny
Existence brings forth surely,
I alone the blame will take!

Why should I someone other
Look to blame? The atoms not seen
Clearly, eternally.
No imagined place to go!

Section 5

A PLACE TO HIDE

A PLACE TO HIDE

The sounds around me whirling
Pretending to be music
Grabbing the attention of my ear.
They're also in sleep heard
Like untuned harps angels play
Pretending to bring peace
After the perturbation of the day
Sometimes to get away
There are afternoon naps
The evenings are quieter
It gives pause for whistling
Whistling keeps me company
It leaves the noise behind
The darkness of sleep
Is the place to hide
From the day's intrusion
All the whirling around me
There're flip flop steps walking
Wanting to keep in step with me
Other disturbance is ignored

BUBBLES

Our inner life is an abyss, deep
Where bubbles of thoughts surface swift, one on top
another—randomly.
Some become images, some become sounds.
Some images become scribbles, some art,
Some sounds become noise, some music,
From this confusion we make meaning.

An abyss is a void, which is another meaning for
 "nothingness".
From nothingness we paint the landscape of our lives,
(So Michelangelo's "Last Judgment" and Beethoven's
 Symphonies!)
Tragedy and misery, and mischief, are the clouds hanging,
which give life feelings.
We are not smart enough to figure where love has come from,
But without it life would be nothing, but all hell! We are the
artists and musicians.
Some of us don't care for all this stuff, we just love life, and all
the fun—regardless!

EXISTENCE IS A MATREX OF IDEAS

What we know is what we know,
And nothing more, it's all in our heads.
We know of certain ideas our minds generate,
But these ideas do not anything represent,
Until they are verified by experiment.
And even so they are our conclusions.

We each live in a bubble of imagination,
We are science fiction writers, and we don't know it.
What we think we know is what we know,
And nothing more, it's all in our heads.
And there is nothing outside of us to prove it.

Existence is matrix of ideas, a reflection from
The kaleidoscope of our imagination,
Every turn is a Quantum leap ever changing.
We will never know more than we can know,
And even of that we are uncertain!

The inconclusiveness of our decisions,
Is what we brag and boast about!

When we delight in the fragrance of a flower,
We condone the flight our senses have taken,
But only the assent of experience is lasting.
In an assumed world of causality what is morality?
Our reality is only what we are experiencing!

Do we really need to pretend:
To know more than we can ever know?

LIVING BY CHOICE POORLY

Liberty has taught us nothing;
Ambition misdirected leads to a dead-end;
Our happiness is by affluence corroded;
Poverty teaches aggression or, resignation,
Hope has never let us down.
They all can be our teachers, if we let them!

But humankind learns, slowly,
Living life by choice, poorly.
Nothing seems to ever change,
Never by God—surely not
By the hot fires of Hell—
Nor, apocalyptical jargon, reprieves!

THE FLAIRS ON THE CACTUS TREE

To escape the ironies of life,
I fled the wild, dirty, crime ridden city streets,
But found myself walking on iron hard deserts
sands, hot under foot.
The air was dry as autumn leaves, and yellow dull.
No birds flying as far as I could see.
No fruits to quench my wrenching thirst, my
purple tongue.
I must have had a dream, God I thought I saw in
a cactus tree,
Flares of light sparkling from the sun on every
leaf I could see.
Nothing else the hot winds brought to my face,
Not to my gaze.
Not a bird or a bee. I have heard of desert bees.
Also, of scorpions, rattlesnakes, and the wasp's
sting.
But none I found roaming the barren hills; I
kicked a stone or two.
Not a grim face from another human being was
there.
I did awake in the middle of the night to the light
of
A hanging moon decorating a desolate horizon;
I waited for the morning star to rise, it comes up
early!
I still feel my face burning, from the flairs on the
cactus tree.
Could this have been an out-of-body experience, I
find myself standing,
With a leaf in my hand and sand in my shoes?

ON MILLION WHATE PAGES

A million white pages to write upon,
More still needed to write my thoughts of you;
Emotions my heart weaves with golden thread,
Tapestries for ever never ending love.

Somewhere along the many scorching lines,
Weak with sorrow and tears I will endure
The affair with life that I did not begin.
Hard I am driven by this life to shine,
Which I do not beg, or expect to lure.

One never loves where love is forced upon.
Who with a wife or husband likes to live,
Who gives joy and happiness at their will?
Nor existence should we expect to trill,
Where hope is portioned out, never filled.

No one really, for sure, wants existing,
Where greed, ignorance, hatred, rules as king.
This is not true love but a fiction fling,
Written on more than a million pages.

In the end it is not love but a lie,
Written on millions, millions of white pages,
With hearts of men, women—children cry!
A story written without end again, again,
Over and over again without end!

NO PRECIPICE FALL

The primordial atom of our being,
Not a blemish has, or precipice fall.
It rolled out with the stars as the big bang,
The foundation of our being to be.

No telescope or microscope can see
Infinity behind the radiant clouds,
Not that special place our ancestors claim,
The cradle of our humanity.

Rhythm of the stars rituals for our minds.
The prophet and the astronomer see
Their images in a reflected pool,
By narcissism the whole world is fooled.

The wonder of our being evolved free.
All our ancestors were but the steps
Developing our humanity,
Instincts turned to intellectuality.

FEEL THE SAND BETWEEN THE TOES

Will you swim with me to shore?
Hold my hands,
Grip the sands
With our spreading toes!
Leave mermaids on rocks sunbathing,
Say goodbye to dauphines dancing,
Smiling awaiting our applause.
Don't scamper back, scared
As little turtles seem to do!
Saying goodbye to mother, the sea,
Don't forget mother she'll always be,
Knowing every wave crest is a kiss,
Only a mother can her children give;
Leave footprints in the sand
As we walk upright ahead,
Climbing the highest mountains
Searching the limitless skies,
Getting lost in the clouds.
Don't forget from this height
To look back to mother, the sea.
As we soar with the Eagles,
High and wide glance back,
Look for the footprints in the sand,
See little turtles scampering back.
Don't forget the feel of the sand
Between the toes!

Section 6

FLYING WITH SEAGULLS

FLYING WITH SEAGULLS

You called for me but I was lost
in thought, but, and far more than that:
My footsteps on the bars of time were trapped,
the sand on the beaches hid my footprints
from my weary mind.
My thoughts were flying, following seagulls
beyond the restless seas—following dreams
call again. Call again, that I may hear your cry.
More than echo through the walls of time,
echoes weaving patterns for my mind.
Make your call this time louder than before,
beyond and about the rolling waves.
I must know you are there to care,
must comprehend the undulation in your voice,
must see the color of your hair.
Thank the waves you are there,
are you the one answering my prayer?

Someone at my home had called before,
I hurried to answer the door!
But no one was standing there,
no shadow was there, seen standing!
I just stood there panting, wondering,
who could that be calling?
Wondering, who that impatient could be,
calling, but not waiting for me?
Wondering was that someone wanting,
to follow the seagulls to sea?
Wanting to find the footprints the sand
was hiding from me?
I just stood there panting, wondering,

who could that be calling—what else,
could the sand be hiding from me?

LOVE THE LEAVES TO BEAR

Women sprouting children everywhere,
Like butterflies alighting from the air.
Gardens of flowers and weeds appear,
Seeds to spread through the stratosphere

There're so many who don't care
How their offspring will ever grow;
Some with tender love will nurture
Every leaf to bear.

Some trample on the weeds in despair.
Weeds cannot be allowed to grow anywhere,
They will choke the flowers by the stem,
We must get rid of them.

Flowers, butterflies and hummingbirds adorn the skies.
The butterfly needs the flower to perch on,
The nectar the hummingbird needs
In the flower bosom lie.

The flower must its petals open
To kiss the hummingbird as it flies.
The flower, butterfly and the hummingbird
Nurse each other with care. The weeds only spread

FISHNETS NYLON KNIT

Fishermen with fishnets nylon knit
cast their nets upon the seas,
fishes caught unexpectedly.
A fathom down little farther
it's hard to see the lights above.
Fishmen nets come empty handed.
Nets not whales made to catch,
only schools of little fishes,
out of school to play.
Nets, seagulls and planes
scare them away,
sharks standby looking for prey.
Seagull and planes overhead flying
the seas have made wavering.
Seagulls diving frighten fishes away,
planes crashing whales aside dashes.
There is no safety in air or sea,
lots of flotsam and debris,
no one is left to swim ashore,
and sigh: "This was not my day!"
Nor, from an island send for help,
S.O.S. Come, I need your aid,
 I am homeless, a castaway!
Fishermen with fishnets nylon knit
ready their nets to cast
must watch the seagulls diving,
see where planes have crashed,
heads above the flotsam bobbing,
souls his nylon net to save.
A glint of Bile stories knit!

WITHOUT A WITNESS STANDING

There're no Philosophic truths,
Only new discoveries.
Moral truths are
Human needs and understanding.
Meaning has no boundary,
Purpose no design,
Without a witness standing.

Definitions are imaginary boundaries,
Tying life's loose ends.
To save my individual sanity,
Loneness, anguish, and doubt
Mustn't be denied—
The existential facts belied!

Rationalism doesn't always make sense,
When reason is dead.
Positivistic, optimistic delusions
Disgraced are now standing,
Alone, in the morning enduring,
I must rise, to meet the emerging sun!

IDEAS IN MY HEAD

Am sorting a few ideas in my head,
To see if I can make poetry of them.
You can help if you care to join.
Society pays bounty in spite of modernity,
A revolution without cause is savagery
To no end.
Every morning breakfast children are fed
A bowl filled with lies and lead,
Sprinkled with prejudice and bigotry heavily,
They are made to believe it's heavenly.
Suicide is a creed that has no reward,
Neither here or in the unforeseen;
Who by force settles an argument?
By force is destroyed—dead!
Collateral damage is not a debt
We co-sign to help a friend,
But assent to destruction
We take no responsibility for.
Friendly fire usually kills bystanders
Who claim to be our friends.
But the justification for our actions
Must be immediately connected
To our survival.
How can we engage in medieval thinking?
Watching Bay Watch on digital TV!
They're cultural clots that have no mind,
But wallow in economic windfalls,
As though it really comes from the sky.
Religious intolerance and racial prejudice
Are banners too often flown
In defense of the slightest assumed offence.

We often with injustice claim others are
Unjust to us, which in effect means we don't
Care for justice as long as we are justified.
Revivalism is trying to resuscitate something
That's long dead. It's not a new mental attitude.
Maybe we should try revitalization,
Or reforestation to avoid starvation.
Evangelical meetings are called revivals,
They are trying to revive the living not the dead.
Revive in them some forgotten creed,
Defend them for their own ends.

Fundamentalists are not fundamental,
Meaning genuine and authentic,
They are without foundation themselves,
They just have these crazy ideas
To tell everyone else they are wrong.
In a global world economy no one lives
Any longer in a secure neighborhood,
But in a gateless community where
Everyone is free to come and go,
That makes us vulnerable to vandalism,
Peeping Toms and serial killers,
With bombs strapped to their bellies.
Sometimes our choices are worse or bad,
But we have no alternatives, but to make them.
We can't avoid the consequences of
Religion and politics, we must pay our fees,
Or the right attention to them.
When we must live with a dilemma,
We must not recriminate ourselves.
The fact is we all do, but have no one
To blame for them, but the sun that shines.
It's hard to avoid clichés,
They are like celebration parades,
They disperse easily when it rains,

But we need the flag waving,
To see children smiling,
The clowns, dogs, and fire engines.
It has something to do with
Unity and Morality.
It's not that I am done,
But when I go, I've gone,
Why would I want to go anywhere
In the same shoes or, the same form,
Or come back to trash the same ears of corn?
My atoms will help to light the stars, and
They're many to take my place and carry on
To finish what I've left undone!
We all complain we don't have the time
To do what we should have done!

ALCHEMIC QUACKERY

In some ancestral alchemic quackery
Alchemists are turning lead into gold
Searching books stolen from eternity
Just to find truth missing in all of them.
Turning lies to truth, a craft we do well.
Touch a switch on the wall dark turns to light,
That is still not the truth we hope to find,
Darkness to light by the wave of the hand.
That's a trick alchemists can never do.
The effects of our technology,
A trick only intelligence can do!

WHY TAKE SO SERIOUSLY OUR

TRADITIONS

Why by our history we're terrified,
Horrified we do not know,
When we were born or we'll die.
We must live, not divine or prophesy.

I must rely on nature's signs,
From the gods of fire or the sun
Standing on the mountain high
Thunderbolt in hand destruction casting.

After reflecting on each generation,
I see they build monuments to them,
Cults joining generation after generation.
Cathedrals built to sacrifice the soul.

Jacob must sacrifice his only son,
A decree by ancient law, not a
Naturalistic or natural conclusion.
Step by step our potential will grow.

Some axioms of our desires,
Cloud storms of emotions drive,
Not the cognitive force producing,
From experience realities of their own.

From experience Humanity is crafted,
Personality is not fixed it's malleable,
For intent and purpose it's an inclination,

An input of culture, growing, not eternal.

Desire drives the patterns of emotions,
Forming our future aspirations.
The mind must apprehend its cognitions,
Where its actions to send and flow.

Why take this untenable position,
Human nature for granted is taken.
Awareness unrestrained by intuition!
Why take so seriously our tradition?

BEING IGNORANT OF IGNORANCE

I was talking with this fellow smoking a big cigar.

He said:
"You know, the problem with the world is ignorance."

Continuing said:
"Yes, its ignorance", puffing on his big cigars.
He said this while the lethal blue smoke swirls around
his head.

I said to him:
Do you think, it's because the ignorant
Are ignorant of their ignorance? —He said, "You are
right!"

I asked him:
Do you think smoking tobacco will hurt you?

He answered:
"No! I have been smoking all my life, love it!"

He said:
"A good cigar is relaxing, it clears my head,
And I can think of all the destructive things in the
world."

He said:
"People think smoking will hurt you,
Why are people so ignorant, I will not stop smoking?"

Not too long after, he was dead never knowing what

killed him.
All his friends after the burial were smoking cigars!

I am wondering, isn't this all so very frightening,
Not being aware of all the ignorance of ignorance? Nor
The ignorant of their own!

II

I was sitting on a parks bench trying to get some fresh air,
Beside me this fellow had five Hamburgers on his lap,
By the empties besides him, he must have drunk gallons
 of pop.

I said to him:
Eating early, it's not lunchtime yet!

He said:
"I eat when I am hungry, and that's all the time."

I said:
Doesn't that make you overweight, bad for your health?

He said:
"I was always big, that's the way I was meant to be,
People think I am fat, but I don't see it that way."

I said:
What do you say to people who call you obese?

He said:
"I tell them they are skinny, get out of my way."

I am wondering, isn't this all so very frightening,
Not being able to change what people think about
themselves.

TRADITIONS WE FOLLOW

We must make up our beds in the morning
If we want to sleep in contort at night.
My father said tradition we fellow:
So we make our beds so we will lie!
This may seem like a good idea today,
When youth by drugs and doctrines stray away.
But whose tradition should lead our way?
There is so much talk about evolution,
Progress contradicts our traditions.
There is tradition of creation,
All things by intelligence designe,
Wants to control their youthful mind.
Where can we find compatibility?
Are those who break away from tradition,
The ones to lead the pack to space and back,
The ones whose tradition we should follow?
My father said tradition we follow:
So we make our beds so we will lie!
We find it hard to make a decision,
Until the morning sunlight we all see,
It will not last for all eternity.
Tradition is only a comfort zone,
So we make our beds so we will lie!

COUNTING THE STARS ONE BY ONE

He died inadvertently,
Counting the stars one by one
To go as far as one can.
The wall of Jericho built,
The tower of Babel climbed,
A confusion of tongues finds.
Believe in Moses' commandments,
Or the equations of Einstein?
The Odyssey of Homer
Tells our destructive side,
The Iliad the Trojan War.
Walls by trumpet calls will fall,
The scripture of crucifixion,
Darwin of evolution.
By deluge all will drown,
With cloudbursts of delusion.
Nowhere dry land to be found,
No support but our own,
We seemed to be lost in space.
He died inadvertently,
Counting the stars one by one
To go as far as one can!

A CON ARTIST

You call me an artist,
Please don't!
I am just man who imitates nature.
Am not just the masterpiece
You think I am.
Fact is, am a thief and a forger;
I have stolen life and think it belongs to me,
And I have forged a dream of heaven!

You call me a master painter,
A maestro composer of music,
A poet—a wizard with the rhyme and rhythm of words,
A scientist who knows it all,
Please don't!

It is the sunshine that paints the landscapes,
The winds that compose the symphonies—
The birds that sing the songs,
It's the rhythm and the rhyme of the seasons
That sustains the harmony of the skies,
I don't!

I wish I knew how to do all theses things,
I don't!

I am just a thief and a forger who steals
The minds and souls of his fellowman;
Just a Con artist who sells at a great price
A forgery of heaven—just a con artist
Who imitates life!

THE OPENNESS I DREAM ABOUT

I have this dream about openness,
It bothers me, wherever I turn I see
Closed doors, windows and jeopardy.
Jealousy and deceit hang like black foam.

I dream of openness,
But not the openness of the deserts
Where rattlesnakes hide.
It's the openness of prairies, grassy tracks of land,
Where we see Buffalos, and Coyotes call home.

I dream of openness,
How deep is the ocean, how high the sky?
It's the openness, which knows no depth, or any height.
This is the openness I dream about.

It's the openness beyond the heavens,
Beyond where the clouds glide,
It's the openness of a mind to another mind,
Where hearts beat together with joy.

I dream of openness,
It's the openness that would allow us
To trust each other, believe the same things.
It's the openness of innocence before
Children are taught to lie.

It's the openness that history hides,
The openness to dare and tell the truth,
Not for gain or loss, but just the truth.
Can we go back to the simplicity

Of being earnest and sincere?
That's the openness I dream about.

HOPE FROM THE DEBRIS

If life over, again we all could live?
Would it be free, conceived, as it should be?
Free the fruit to eat from all the trees I see.
Free from the promise of Heaven, from Hell!
Free from all economic oppressions,
From all evil, from all bigotries spell!.

Resources topping, Poet I would be.
I would the rhythm and the rhymes of life find;
I would the rivers let flow where they will,
The sunshine free, on the daffodils;
Would the mountains roam, live the valleys low.
That's the vision of the world poet willed!

The evil we have conceived, we don't see,
It spreads as all wildfires do, uncontrolled!
Emotions unasserted held,
Intellects smoldering under the smog,
The hearts that would for life aspire, clog.
But from all the debris hope emerges, still!

Seriously, the question we all must ask,
How long, quenching forest fires, can we live?
Should we perchance fully this insight gain:
(Along with the ever-revolving sun
And the caressing light of a new moon)
Every dawn to us gives a new life to live!

O! By the rising sun, again, redeem!

HOPE IS MORE THAN A DREAM

There is no doubt, am awed by all I've seen.
Some say there is something that intervenes,
Between the things seen and the things unseen.
In fact, many say it is "That" of which
The skies, fishes of the sea, the birds on trees
Are made. No doubt they are of something made!
But there are many skeptics' doubts—
They take for granted a Creators Dream.

They do by rays of light miracle shout!
By virgins' halos claim a Savior comes!
Some cannot find hope in things they don't see.
And doubt the songs they hear of birds on trees.
They don't for the rains care, the sun despair!
Life they claim, a mistake that needs repair.

Most lose hope with all their acquisition.
Ambition blinds their sense of right from wrong.
But hope is more than a dream of things seen;
Hope guides aspirations to completion,
When on o'r expectations we falter.
Some don't stop trying all life to alter.

Don't be disappointed in what I say
For as poet I must sing, hope to bring.
Don't be disillusioned with things I sing,
As poets must bring hope for all to win.
Don't question the things we see, what we don't!
Live your dream; it's never late, life to take.

I would sing today of hope to love wed.

Hope and love are the invisible threads
That bind together the sinews of life.
They are of that intuitive wisdom,
Which drives us to find love before we're dead,
Love is an experience only lovers share,
Hope the foundation of our prayers.
Without hope and love life's ills are nightmares!

Many doubt, hope and love are spiritual

LOVE IS METHAPHYSICAL

Love is Metaphysical,
Of which many a treatise has been written,
But when you take it out the dryer
After its been washed,
It collapses to a feeling,
Hard for us to define.

Many claim they wear it,
And try to show it off,
In fact they parade it for all to see:
In tuxedos and fancy wedding gowns.
When you come right down to it,
It wears better in dungarees and coveralls.

Love is Metaphysical,
Very hard to understand,
When you come right to it,
We have to work at it, to make it work.
Humans have been working at it,
For centuries to no end.

Stories of famous love have been told,
But history lies for no one,
It has never hidden poor results:
Cupid, Abelard and Helios, Anthony and Cleopatra,
They all ended in tragedy or in war.
Love is no easy feeling, hard to understand.

On the other hand, love may be Theological.
We must leave some things for God to do,
Human's interfering the work He has to do,

For once, Let Him do what He does best:
Rid the world of hatred and the dirty stuff,
Fill the human heart with feelings called love!

SEX IS SEX

Sex is sex, and love is love,
When they meet, they compliment.
Neither can be mistaken for the other.
Sex is like music, love more like prayer.
Rock music doesn't appease the spirit
As Gregorian chants, or a little hymn;
For entertainment symphonies are pleasing

The social gospel of the streets,
Out bound the restraints of liberty,
With delinquent tones of rap,
And erotic words of intent:
Spasm of passion, climax and orgy.

Rap as rap, is amusing, needn't be educational.
Music can be elevating, as well as depraving.
Sex mustn't be considered recreational,
Nor mistaken for love.

The expression of love is love, of sex desire,
Sex has one end love has none?
Sex violates the bounds of cultural authority,
Love upholds the mores of society

Section 7

CHILDREN LEARNING TO FLY

CHILDREN LEARNING TO FLY

Children always want to fly.
Don't we all? Don't know why?
Fantasies or fanaticism emerging like storms,
No calm seen ahead brewing,
Never calm, only storms;
In the morning like water bubbling
Hot for coffee. Never calm!
The turmoil in my head.
Morning ebullience, no evidence,
One bubble after another dead.
Ebullience respects no more,
All is ebullience. Prejudice!
What we are taught to see is red.
Everywhere yards and yards of gray thread,
Like knotted tendrils in the head.
No sentry at the gate, we are led
Where neurotransmitters exchange
Love for hatred.
Only graveyards of gray matter where
Love is dead.
Children always want to fly,
Never learned. Don't know why!

FOR THE CHILDREN

My lamentations are not for the dead,
Nor, for those who pretend to be my friend,
Nor, for the promise of scriptures shed!

My dead to me in memory very dear,
In that state of peace, don't need my prayer.
It's the injustice of life we should fear!

Optimistically, I reconciled,
But only anguish in my heart I find;
Despair, the hunger cry in every child!

Despair, indifference of the ruling class,
Longing to know from them the truth at last,
Longing to find my way out of confusion!

Sometimes, I pretend in my delusion,
At last I have found the right faith, or friend.
This will be my aspiration to the end!

With deceit and deception don't befriend,
Don't the heart of a child with hatred fill—
The wonders of the stars, the heavens sing!

Perhaps, God His grace to all children brings!
I wait! I wonder sometimes very tall;
Am I the one chosen whom it befalls?

IT'S THE CHILD IN US

In the heart of every man cries
Are heard at dawn since time began,
Yearnings louder than any sigh,
Reverberating crawling steps
Of the child almost lost in time.
The man is but the child he was
Crawling on the floors of heaven,
He grasps at all moving objects
Pushing higher to grasp some more.
The child in us is never lost,
It's the sigh we hear everywhere,
It's the sleepless winter nights awake
Waiting for Santa Claus to come.
It's the children who don't let us
Forget every day is today,
To cry at our parents' death,
At our daughter's wedding day.
It's the child in us that must play
The game, forget the tragedy!

THE VIRTUE IS IN THE CHOOSING

If it's right because it gives pleasure,
And wrong because it gives pain;
Is it oblivion when neither is manifest?

The horizon is where the eye stops seeing,
It's not where the sea meets the sky.
Can't you tell reality from dreaming?

The vanity of self-possessions is a mirror
Where those who hunger for appraisal
May be seen to prosper by the illusion.

II

The thing, which sets me off in this direction—
In choosing I had to break my ties!
The road didn't end at the fork,
One may become two or two may end as one.
But mine is the choice to make,
Wherever I am headed—I didn't mean
To be set apart.
The virtue is in the choosing,
Can't you understand!

WISDOM IS EVER SO KIND

Wisdom has been ever so kind,
But it has yet to prove
It can overcome illusion.

Wisdom must prevail
For it is from ignorance
That evil springs.

Wisdom always accompanies
A rising sun, but it is
In the illusive shadows
That ignorance hides.

Take away the blocks,
Where there are now shadows,
Pure light shines—so does wisdom!

You can change your life,
Only one thought at a time,
So the world—that's wisdom!

TODAY WE LIVE

Yesterday and tomorrow
Extensions in imaginary time.
Yesterday is lost to today
Tomorrow we yet to find.
No yesterdays or tomorrows
Will do what today can.
Today is such a short time
Blink of an eye it's gone.
Who can tell we lived
When it's all gone.
Nothingness is important
Only to those who live.
Yesterday forever is gone
Tomorrow never comes in time
Today is the only time to live.
Today is the only day
We all can count on.
Live today the way we should
Or might as well be dead.

CLIMBING UP A HILL

Climbing up a hill for no good reason,
Just a climbing will.
The earth I stepped upon rolled down
The hill for no good reason.
I increased my steps faster one by one,
The intent was to reach the summit of my will,
And leave the valleys of hell far away below.
Rocks I stepped upon rolled down the hill one by one,
There were cries for help, for me to halt, going up the hill.
I paused for a moment trying to feel someone's pain,
But could not stop, going higher up the hill,
Every step brought me closer to my destination.
The higher I went the harmony of the skies I heard.
Never my intent peacefulness to break where I've gone.
To integrate with all, as far as I can see, and beyond.
To Heaven I really want to go, comprehend what is told.
On my way up a crow flew close by, very bold,
It crowed, in many languages said goodbye.
The sound forlorn an omen of things to come,
I froze my steps and looked all around,
Cause unseen, something, wants my soul to die.
It matters not, for I think I was, by a miracle saved.
A few steps closer to Heaven now, my hands I wave.
I can tell for the sun is brighter all around
And helped my approach with every step I made
The crow flew far away, below, and I am climbing
Higher. One step higher up the hill

A HAND WAVING AT ME

The winds blind my eyes with passing fury,
The clouds rush by with total disregard.
My eyes flashed fire, as sapphires
Light the sky. Passing past the horizon.

Sea waves rising and falling went their way,
Hard as I tried I could not catch the wind.
The clouds were changing form so rapidly,
There was no time to see a face at bay.

My eyes did start a fire in the sky,
And I saw a sail not too far away.
My mind had stirred with illusion before,
Can I trust my senses were there a sail?

Am trying to find my way back to land,
I was lost between the sky and the sea;
Extending my hands to touch the winds, the clouds,
I saw the sail, hands waving back to me!

We sailed together towards the shore,
Passing past the horizon the sun went;
Joyful a gale has passed no harm done,
We sat watching the skies sapphire lit!

ANGELS AT THE DOOR

It was some felicitous turning,
Which led me to your door.
I need not look high and low
For the nook you are hiding.

It was a beam of light from your window,
Casting a shadow outdoors,
A shadow only is all I knew,
Until I knocked and you opened the door.

It was some felicitous turning
When I found your heart was open.
It was like a stroke of lightning
Revealing a hidden destiny, but foretold.

I was out walking looking at the stars,
Some secret longing led me to your window;
I thought I saw the silhouette of an angel.
It was you waiting for my knock on the door.

How could I have missed you before?
I have walked pass your window
Many nights, no one was there standing;
Some felicitous turning—angels at the door!

THE LOVE OF LIFE

The images in my mind are pictures of you,
Landscapes in which with arms open,
You are running towards me;
They are as repetitious as the beat of a heart:
My mind and my heart consequently,
Are the suns and moons of your life
Revolving constantly.
My mind is always thinking and
My heart racing towards you,
As planets attract one another to balance the stars.
Sometimes we're close as two apples on a tree,
At times, as far as oceans can part.
The "I" of my mind and the "Thou" of your heart
Are seeking to merge as one absolute love
No one can part.
Why I am and you came to be,
The mystery supreme no one can solve,
You are my thoughts and yours of me;
But for our love there is no eternity.
We must revolve with the planets eternally!

NO ONE WANTS TO BE ALONE

Somehow I am thinking today is tomorrow.
Why I am confused this late in life having so
Little left, and not having much in the first place?
What is past went so fast no time to remember,
Months quickly flying, every month is December.

It was yesterday I was but a child playing,
In glutted city blocks and muddy city streets.
Not afraid what my father would say, I had none,
My mother she is working long days, very late.
I am lonely my loneliness never leaves me.

It's the feeling of being alone roaming the sky,
It's the only company I've had these many years.
Like a scar I have on my thigh from falling.
A child with a pair of crutches limping along
Not eliciting much pity from anyone.

Childhood can be rough, but we don't know about it
Until we are grown, all we feel is scars of pain.
And we wonder why we feel so strange no one cares.
No one wants to share my pain, or take any blame
Everyone pretends they do not see the shadows

Under my eyes. They should know am waiting for love.
Shadows keep me company wherever I go,
They follow like a portrait of a grandmother
I never knew. Died giving birth to my mother.
All mothers have their scars and pain they must bear.

No one wants to be alone as a child, or grown,
We need to find our ancestral roots and ties.
We will search all the birth records and history books,
Climb mountains, and dive to the bottom of the sea.
I didn't know my grandmother she died before me.

That doesn't mean I must stop searching, keep searching;
Her portrait lingers wherever I seem to go,
It's somewhat reassuring to know she was very
Elegant. A woman of some stature perhaps,
An inspiration to defeat all poverty!

WHERE IS THE GUIDE GUIDING US

When did we fall below the snow?
Where is the guide guiding us, we must know,
Why he'd led us to the precipice?
Who is this guide guiding us?
Why did he leave us with no place to return!
No certain way to find
Our way back home!

AT THE END OF THE DAY

Because I was born today,
This is not the only day I'll have,
It is the first, certainly not the end.

Nor the place I was born
The only place I'll ever have,
Nor the only place I'll ever be.

All leaves must fall,
They seem to go wherever they will,
Gently falling with the help of the wind.

The creeping grass below must be still,
Forming beds for falling things,
The growing grass comforts so many things.

Because I was born today,
Doesn't mean there are no tomorrows,
The place I was born isn't the end of destiny.

At the end of the day we find all tomorrows,
We must not be weighted down
By the sorrows of today, all the little things.

At the end of the day is where tomorrow begins,
Where the day ends is where
The rainbows all begin.

Today is the ground we stand on,
The future is the dream we depend on!

Section 8

BEFORE WE DIE

BEFORE WE DIE

The things we do and say before we die,
In life we all know our beginning,
but no one knows the reason why we are born.
We know where we are born, the time and year;
parents tell us about our childhood,
and about our growing up antics.

But we'll never know where, how, when, we'll die.
This is one of the many mysteries of
our lives we are forbidden to know.
There're also circumstances and events
occurring, changing the course we will take,
no fortuneteller's Crystal Ball foretells.

We are vulnerable and it's easy
to let go, be carried by the flow
of life, be crushed on the rocks.
Be bruised by the curves we are dashed against.
A lesson we can learn from the Beaver,
with twigs and bushes, persistent he builds

a dam against the mighty rivers.
If we are to avoid being crushed against
the river of life, we must slow the speed
of the current life we are living.
We're not sure why we were born or will die,
our life, we are sure we can enjoy!

LETTER TO A FRIEND

When I sat to write this letter to you
My friend,
I thought I had a lot to say,
And so it'll turn out to be;
We have so much to reminisce,
'Bout our youthful days:

The pranks we played with girls' pick tails;
The ink I spilled on your coveralls;
How the teacher you jinxed with
Your fingers crossed;
The frog we put on her desk, that fall;
The birds we watched to steal their eggs;
The candies we stole,
From Mr. Bens' food store.

Now we are both full grown and tall,
It's time to mend a broken heart,
It's time to tell and spill it all:
You must know the girl you married,
You stole from me.
She was my best gal, preferred of all.
You did not know my heart or intent,
That's why you are still my best friend.

After all that was a long time ago!
Now I sit on my porch pipe in hand,
And watch others children play football.

All your children love me too,
And are beautiful to look at.

I love them as much as any
I would have got.

But I must say with a heart so full,
I wondered what feature they would have
If I had fathered them, one and all.
For some unknown reason I Reminisce,
Can't forget you all,

Your best of friends.

PS
We must wonder:
What grip is this that grips us all?
The good and the bad, the small and tall,
That drives to search for something more in life,
Beyond the child, beyond the wife, beyond the grave!

THE CONSEQUENTIAL

To many,
The inconsequential may be butterflies
Flirting with one another in the sky.
Can our joys be inconsequential?
Can the things that give us love be mental?

Are the continents continental?
Or, just the people living on them?
Are flying airplanes any better,
Than the winds that sustain them?

It's compliments that fill the heart with joy.
The consequence of compliments never
Are inconsequential to our lives.

Butterflies and birds flying compliment
The sunshine and the clouds in the sky,
If the sky stops raining, the earth will dry.
Mothers feed their children till breasts run dry.

Nothing in life is inconsequential,
There're many things that makes our hearts sigh.
Hatred is not complimentary,
Love's consequential to humanity!

LOOK AT THE SKY

The clouds were rolling behind me,
Faster than our minds could see.
If it were left to me, I would
Slow the winds down, more faces make,
Let the radiance of the sun burst
Through as eyes of love recognized.

These clouds at times seem so friendly,
At times they frown with brows made up.
It seems that all humanity
They want to scowl for forgetting
To look at them, to see the sun
Shining, through them year in and out.

It's not only the clouds and sun
We are forgetting as we go
Speeding the highways recklessly,
But, most importantly how, why
They are there for eternity?
Before we leave, look at the sky!

JUST KEEP DREAMING

I used to be some kind of an idealist,
I believed in all kinds of funny stuff,
Until one morning I awoke to know
The difference of a nightmare from a dream.

I was never a materialist for I knew
That nothing is real and lasting in a dream,
Nor in the Universe we take as solid to stand on,
But it was the nightmare that got me thinking.

If things are so horrifyingly real in a nightmare,
What is the difference between reality and a dream?
For we know that in reality nothing is solid
Or lasting, the same as in the dream.

So between reality and dreaming
Everything seems what in reality it is not.
This unreality about reality got me thinking:
If life is just a dream, and then the future would be
but a lie?

I am neither an Idealist nor materialist any longer,
I dropped all the funny stuff, and have nothing solid
or lasting to stand on.
I am wondering what to depend on if everything is
but a lie?
The best is to just keep dreaming and have an open
mind!
Nightmares do not last forever!

IS IT A DREAM

I want to share with you this feeling,
It's the feeling where poetry comes from,
The feeling spring brings after winter is gone.

It's seen, heard and tasted in many words,
Felt by all the poems ever written.
It is in the flowers in paradise,
In all the heavens we have ever dreamed,
It's in the language of every scripture.

It cannot really be described.
If dearly we call it spiritual,
We give it a dimension and a name.
That would be a shame, if that's all we would feel.

There is no dimension or name,
To what I want to share with you,
It eludes all the words we have written,
It's just a feeling I must share with you.

We speak of love when love we do not know,
For love is that mystery behind the stars,
It hides the scars, life for us to enjoy.

If name we give it, be it love and hope
For they are dimensionless that's for sure.
Love and hope are the feelings to convey,
Without these "feelings" life wouldn't endure.

Many say it's only a dream,
be it only a dream

We all need love and hope,
to keep us company!

After all we say, life is a drama,
Only in poetry we can best express.

THIS EUPHORIC FEELING

This euphoric feeling I have,
Moving through space and space through me,
Above the elation birds must feel
Borderless flying eternally.

The skill of engineers haven't
Discovered the equation of
Infinity without boundary,
The dynamics of this flying,

Nor of this ebullient feeling,
Which within our souls hide?
Conjure of inquisitive minds.
Boundless it is when we are still.

In the night our souls are heard
Crying, flying with angels' wings,
Ever searching volumes of clouds
To find this euphoric feeling.

Most pervading when we are still!
When mostly it's needed it hides,
When the least expected it slides
Out the night to stop our cries.

LIFE FREELY GIVEN

Thanks for the life I have,
The life you have freely given.
I don't question why birds fly,
Why the clouds come freely and go,
Wherever they may choose to hide.
Why the sands and the seas are revered;
And some the core of life despise.
I know conscious life is precious,
Without it we wouldn't know were are here.
My mind with gratitude opens as a flower,
The wellsprings of my heart to wonder,
Why I have this sense of someone standing
Watching every step I take with care,
It helps me with the chores and storms
Which faith may blow my way.
There are no questions in my heart,
But acceptance without condition
Of this life I have, freely given!

THE FINAL PROCLAMATION

When the final proclamation is made
About the freedom of the human race
The first article to be stated, is to free them
From the beast within.

The second, is to state clearly
Who and what are these gods that scare them?

The third is, how to stop deceiving their fellowmen,
And down the line we must define,
Why through the centuries they have lied to themselves,
How to break these lies of our ancestry?

The truth eludes them and justice is never clear.
What is justice, and when is justice ever served?

Why do they out-rightly deny their right to be free?
Their human right to be, not for any reason
But just to inhale the salt air from the sea.

They've lost their sense of right and wrong and of beauty,
Denying the laws of casualty.

As faith is not an alternative to reason,
They are not clear which rules to obey,
The rules of Athens or Jerusalem?

Science has not been able to teach them
What reality really is! So far
We are at ground zero, nothing for sure as yet.

And when they kill themselves and others
With atrocious crimes, such as:
Political corruption, religious deception,
Or plain outrageous senseless wars,
They go into self-denial, never admit they are wrong!

When will we start writing this ultimate proclamation
To stake our human rights, and respect for our humanity?
The deceleration of independence of the human race,
Is the declaration to be free from, ignorance, greed and
 hatred.

How long are we to endure this perennial self-denial?

Will we ever eliminate the scourge war?
Define and ensure human rights,
Uphold worldwide the rule of law,
And foster for all, social and economic development?

WISDOM, LOVE AND HOPE

The intellect and emotions
Are both the oceans,
The depth from which
Rise the power of wisdom and love.
Wisdom and love are self-sufficient
Unto their subjects, unto themselves,
They need nothing to compliment them.
Neither have a beginning nor an ending,
Nor a shape or a form.
They are the beginning and the end,
They shape and they form all
We know and love thru them.
They are as humble as a bee
As powerful as all the oceans can be.
Neither contends nor pretends
To be greater than the other.
But they are the forces that can
Conquer ignorance and hatred.
The wisdom of Sophia and the love of Aphrodite
Are gifts to mankind from the heavens and the seas!
From the goddesses of wisdom and love,
The mystery of hope their offspring must be!

THE NOSTALGIC DAY WHERE IT ALL

BEGAN

I am a human in stages of disrepair,
Age has taken hold by decree.
I've never reached the perfection of a sphere,
My recall is faltering, my memory is fading too.

Each face but reflects the phase of an ideal,
Once, I aspired to be a Prophet, or
Perhaps a Philosopher or a King.
But, I can hardly see the shadows in
The footsteps of a hiding moon.

I was never one to live in a moral cage,
Nor by vague chains of ethics be restrained.
Yet my life was good, a standard set—
Never one to fall from—self-contained.

The wife I had was there for me,
And so my many children too.
Along the way I've made a friend, and
Perhaps more than just a few.

Barely recovering the hope in my despair,
I've never planted a tree, but wrote a book,
In the many pages I strove, and wrote
What was hard for some to see
The mysteries of life in a leaf from a tree.

"That" was then, now am here,
In this stage of disrepair;
No longer seeing the road ahead, or where it ends,
But somehow still remembering, vaguely,
The nostalgic day, where it all begins.

GRAND FINALE

IN SLEEP WE CEASE FIRE

The windows of the night
Through which in sleep we peek
At another dimension of time
Opens to all possibilities of heaven.
This is where we find the limitlessness
Of the human mind.
We can see the gate beyond all faiths
Through which our minds can slip
Infinitely, eternally beholding the absolute.

This is where all the gods dwell
Beyond all the hell we've made of earth.
If we can lose our anger and hatred in sleep,
And get a taste of heaven, isn't it time
We reconcile and live heavenly on earth?

Night and sleep is the common ground—
The gateway where differences are lost,
And the Oneness of our being desegregates,
And differences of opinion are superficial.
Sleep has always been the gateway to heaven,
The foundation of our aspirations and our dreams.
We should be thankful to the gods who let us sleep!

Are we destined to be somnambulating?
It's only in sleep, we "Cease Fire"!
If our faith has failed us,
Shouldn't we bring forth a "New Gospel"
From the windows of the night?

OUR PREDILECTIONS

How we predicate our ideas
To our own predilections!
Even the will of God we bend.

We write our Philosophies
Telling God what He should become,
And what He should do and not do.

We don't care about all the destruction
We've caused to God and our fellowman,
Only our predilections matters.

Many ideas are like serpents
Seething underbrush thru history's jungles
Swallowing their prey, their bite is lethal,

Becoming the Pythons of social constriction,
Their stronghold strangling human progress:
Poisoning the minds of the religious
Conservatives and economic liberals—

Roots of religion, political corruption —
Statism rampant on the home front
Leading to moral and economical failure;
All the dreams of building magnificent nations,
And all the hope of world peace, shattering.

INDOLENT AND INDOLGENT

Indolent and Indulgent
Pretension led to deception
Easily abdicating responsibility.

We care not for the truth,
If a lie is our intention.
Our lie is the assumption,
That life doesn't belong to us.

If it's not our responsibility,
Why shouldn't we live
Indolent and indulgent?

Egos are parading
In self-made costumes of pretension,
Bystanders participating in the charade.

The face is yours,
Where does the mask come from?
Deceit is what you hide
The truth cannot be hidden.
All pretension
Is the ego parading?

The proof is what you see,
Not what you have to prove.
Look quietly at the little flower
Clinging on the crag, growing fearlessly
On that ominous mountainside.

ABOUT THE AUTHOR

Thomas P. Lind is retired; he was Director of Dietary
Services at The New York United Hospital Medical Center
of Port Chester, N. Y., where he also taught classes in
Biofeedback theory and practice at the school of
Encephalography. He has degrees in Psychology. He was
a member of the International College of Applied Nutrition
and of the American Hospital Association, and an
associate member of the Academy of Orthomolecular
Psychiatry. He was a member of the American Association
of Sex Educators, Counselors and Therapists of Washington,
D.C., and is a Certified Sex Therapist. He holds a
certificate in Rational-Emotive Counseling from The
Institute for Advanced Study in Rational Psychotherapy,
chartered by the Regents of the University of the State
of New York.
Other works: GREEN IS THE GARDEN, a volume of
Poems; THE FACTS OF LIFE YOU ARE BEING
DENIED, none-fiction, a philosophical/psychological
approach to life. AN EPIC OF THE MIND. IF THE
HEAVEN BREAK OPEN. BEGGING THE
QUESTION. FLYING WITH SEAGULLS.